Devonport Maid

By

Lizzie Khalil

Warning and Consideration
Some content may unintentionally offend.
This document contains historical accounts of sexual violence, descriptive references to racism, violence, alcohol and substance abuse, offensive language, childhood sexual abuse and references to suicide. Suitable for 18+

Edited By Brian R Eldred 2024-2025

Book cover By Ira 2024

Illustration By Freya R Beavis 2024

Life story of a Devonport Maid

The book charts the true-life story of Lizzie, an unwanted, tiny, black baby girl who was unceremoniously abandoned at birth by her delinquent teenage mother, Shirley Rose, who left her in a predominantly white town and her fight of coming to terms with her lot after being dumped on her racist family.

After surviving years of relentless bullying and racial abuse Lizzie found herself the master of her own destiny, deciding she had one of two choices: either sink or swim.

After a DNA test revealed the shocking and earth-shattering truth about her "deliberately hidden beginnings" Lizzie, using all the wit and cunning that she had learned surviving on one of England's most brutal council estates, decided it was time to swim faster than she'd ever done before!

Join Lizzie on her brutally honest true-life story and her long journey fraught with lots of tears and buckets of laughter on this you-couldn't-make-it-up, funny and very personal and sometimes shocking tale of self-discovery, determination, loss, and true love.

Table of Contents

Chapter One 10

DNA 10

Chapter Two 23

Not Once, But Twice. 23

Chapter Three 27

Abracadabra 27

Chapter Four 31

Blanche 31

Chapter Five 38

The Breakup 38

Chapter Six 40

Beauty Tips 40

Chapter Seven 51

The New King 51

Chapter Eight 58

The King is dead 58

Chapter Nine 63

The End of Nathan 63

Chapter Ten 69

The Visit 69

Chapter Eleven 71

Ass Kicking Time 71

Chapter Twelve 73

Ballistic Missile 73

Chapter Thirteen 78

College Days 78

Chapter Fourteen.. 83

Roxanne 83

Chapter Fifteen... 88

Cardiff Born 88

Chapter Sixteen.. 94

Welsh and Gran.. 94

Chapter Seventeen 100

What could go wrong? 100

Chapter Eighteen.. 105

Final Destination!... 105

Chapter Nineteen 131

It's nothing... 131

Twenty 133

Bad feelings 133

Chapter Twenty One... 143

Goodbye... 143

Chapter Twenty Two 145

After the Storm, Cold Rain 145

Chapter Twenty Three 156

Young again!.. 156

Chapter Twenty Four 160

Little Yellow Hobo 160

Chapter Twenty Five.. 165

Never in a million years... 165

Chapter Twenty Six 172

Thunderclap and Lightning OMG! 172

Chapter Twenty Seven.. 176

No rest for the wicked.. 176

Chapter Twenty Eight.. 179

The Interview.. 179

Chapter Twenty Nine... 197

Like it or lump it.. 197

Chapter Thirty... 207

Gran…again! 207

Chapter Thirty One 218

Friendship 218

Reflections 244

Acknowledgements and Thanks

I'd like to take this opportunity to thank the many people involved in the making of this book. Starting with the obvious, and my biggest supporter, my husband Craig who I refer to as the Welshman throughout this book. Thank you for always loving me. X

My three childhood friends, Jilly, Stella and last, but not least Judith., Special thanks to Judi's husband, Paul. He sent me such kind words of encouragement when I first started this venture. Thank you for being part of my story. X

I'd like to thank my old school friends Anne Kamara and Jane Archer, for literally dragging me back to normality. By cleaning me up after my exit from ICU Derriford Hospital. By reminding me that dying was no excuse for looking bad, especially for a Devonport Maid. Thank you for the kick up my ass. X

To Jul Sym thank for just being there it helped me through those long nights when I didn't think I would ever walk again. X

To my cousins Kathy Boydell and Maria Walters, for being so patient with my sometimes judgemental attitude towards our family, and trusting me to do the right thing in the end. Thank you for trusting me girls. X

And the multitude of my old school friends who have shown their support over the past months and to the many, many others, who without them entering into my life, I would not be who I am today. Thank you for being my friends. X

Most of all I would like to thank my children Dean, Marc, Tamsin, Shannon, and baby Freya, who is now 30. Whose existence prompted me to write this book, warts and all. It was them who gave me the idea to chronicle my good times as well as bad, as a part of our family heritage. To help them understand that this story does not end with me and it's for them and my grandchildren to pick up the gauntlet to continue our history.

Then under the strict instructions of our grandmother Granny Blanche, who I've dedicated this book to, because she was the one who said," You're only dead as long as you're forgotten".

Special thanks to my inspiration and teacher our Granny Blanche...

Chapter One

DNA

I always believed the best way to tell the story is to start at the very beginning. In my case, the beginning is a complete and utter mystery. Where I come from they'd say "I don't have a chuffing Scooby Doo" meaning clue?

But here goes…

I thought of many ways to tell this story without rambling on and boring the reader to distraction, but in the end it's my story, and why on earth would anybody else be interested? Unless of course they've found them self in the same predicament as me. I suppose the thirst for knowledge about oneself is a little bit like substance dependency, like the need for that first coffee in the morning, you won't die without it you just want it, it starts your day it gives you the boost you need to tackle the trials and tribulations of the day ahead. I almost feel like 'bullet pointing' my discoveries, and then writing 'The End'! Just to get this bloody mess over with!

I've been told writing one's feelings down is therapeutic, I truly don't believe I need therapy. But others would probably disagree so here goes, I'll start my story here!

Cornwall, England, in the present day.

It's been 12 months since I took that damned DNA test and found out I wasn't the person I always believed I was!

I was born in Plymouth, a historic naval town on the banks of the River Tamar, which borders Cornwall. It was pretty obvious to anybody who came in contact with me that I was not completely indigenous to these lands, dark skinned, thick lips and frizzy hair was it damn good indication that I had black Negro, blood in me. But try telling that to my very English family ha ha..! In fact, they would've battered the living daylights out of anyone who had the audacity to suggest I could be black, myself included.

My heritage was a closely guarded, secret and a secret that the majority of my family took to their grave. Like many families, 'skeletons in the closet' was a way of life, with the door firmly shut tight. As the years passed, and I grew older. I occasionally asked questions like, why is my skin darker, why is my hair so curly? Cornering certain weaker members of my family, a picture then started to form. I was told mum married an African gentleman presumably some kind of a Prince but who knows? But they split up. He went back home and that was it! It took me years of digging, cornering and tricking certain members of the family into spilling the beans, especially when they had a drink or two, which in my family's case was more than often!

I was raised by my grandmother I'd like to say she was formidable. However, she was one of 14 children. She was timid after suffering years of mental and physical abuse by her drunk, autocratic father. He had worked in the harsh environment of the Plymouth fishing boat industry.

Undiagnosed eye problems, left her practically blind, the knock on effect of not being able to see left her practically illiterate.

She suffered horrible bullying. I remember her tearing up one day, telling me her nickname as a child was 'Goo-goo eyes'. My poor gran but, instead of turning her bitter at the world actually this hardship produced a kind person with a big heart and loads of empathy for others me especially, she believed everybody makes mistakes, and everybody deserves a second chance, it's probably the only thing I inherited from my grandmother (Blanche) who I was unceremoniously dumped on at birth. My delinquent teenage mother 16 year old (Shirley Rose) was having none of it. In other words, she didn't want me. However, Shelley had completely vindicated herself and saved the family name from disgrace, by becoming a married woman.

My racist family even accepted that a black husband was far better than the disgrace of having no husband at all! My mother became Mrs Abdul Khalil, the wife of an African academic economic student from the Sudan. That was my reality, my life growing up into adulthood, dreaming that one day this man will come back on a white charger looking for me. However, I eventually give into the realisation I was going to stay fatherless for the rest of my life, resigning myself to the fact that what's done is done, crack on and get on with my life.

As the years passed, I repeated the story to every person who was interested and who questioned my exotic looks, my mother even provided me with a photograph of her and my father on their wedding day, which I have treasured all my life, very often studying and scrutinising the picture, looking for similarities with my children. Believing at least Mr Khalil would live on in the blood of his descendants, my children. Five in total, three boys and two girls from different relationships. I'm afraid the apple didn't fall far from the tree and I inherited my mother's delinquent ways. My 'do what I want' attitude which left me unsettled for years.

Cursed in my youth with my mother's quick wit and good looks, I never had a problem choosing which man was going to spoil me next. In fact, looking back, I was bloody arrogant, spoilt and selfish. I now realise I broke many hearts in the pursuit of me! But everybody meets their match, I will eventually settle down with one man who fits me perfectly. He treats me like a queen, and I love him for it. In other words, we get on like peas and carrots a perfect symbiotic relationship. I give him what he needs and he returns the compliment, absolutely no need to tell of our great love story.

I believe if you have to tell a love story, you're not living in a love story so we will leave it there. I am loved, I am cherished I am blessed. The years past my children grow into adults producing children of their own, there's an old saying your son is your son till he takes a wife, but your daughter is your daughter for the rest of your life! My girls have stayed close. My boys moved on two of them met good women and forged families of their own but that's of no interest to the reader. However, my eldest daughter who may I add is auditioning constantly as head of the family is very attentive every year birthday and Christmas. She likes to get me something special. She knows I'm a bit strange so the ordinary bunches of flowers, or a box of chocolates is wasted on me. My personality can sometimes borderline eccentricity. Last year she provided me with a DNA test.

I've often wondered if my father married again and the thought of me having half siblings from his union with another woman after my mother filled my dreams. But those sorts of unions are what dreams are made of, and something you see in magazine articles and YouTube videos under the heading, "I found my lost family" very often happening to others, but never you. Nice things never happened to me unexpectedly, or out of the blue, did they?

The absolute unquestionable DNA evidence: you've been warned! Many people believe that American biologist James Watson and English physicist Francis Crick discovered DNA in the 1950s. In reality, this is not the case. Rather, DNA was first identified in the late 1860s by Swiss chemist: Friedrich Miescher. Regardless, whoever was first they stirred up a right bloody hornets' nest, because DNA doesn't lie, people make mistakes, but the science is infallible, modern DNA Companies like Ancestry DNA and My Heritage DNA, work on the scientific principle of centimorgans basically for us mere mortals it means the more centimorgans or CM's we share with a person the closer we are related. Can tell if you're a parent or grandparent a half sibling or sibling, aunts uncles, and cousins of various degrees.

The amount of horror stories of families who have opened their DNA results at the Christmas dinner table, for a bit of fun. Only to find out that the children are the milkman's offspring are rising into the thousands! Stories of people who have absolutely no genetic link to their family whatsoever, with proof of a birth certificate showing they are not adopted? How? After investigation, the families left horrified, realising that the babies were swapped at birth by incompetent nurses, are on the rise. In fact, instead of joyful reunions, which do happen, may I add; horror stories of complete family breakdowns, because of DNA truths are rising exponentially. So be warned, because as the old saying goes, "it takes a wise child to know its own father" Something I was soon to discover!

One or two rubs on the inside of your mouth of a cotton bud, a few weeks wait and that was it. A bright future would be laid out in front of me. I fantasised relatives would be queueing up, ready to welcome me with open arms, what I hadn't accounted for was it incredibly slow pace of the American postal system. At first, I thought the tracking page provided was going to be a handy tool. In fact, it turned out to be torture, watching my little animated truck parked up dockside. For days on end, going back and forwards and appeared to be stranded in the Atlantic Ocean at one point! In fact, after about 18 days I gave up, the novelty had worn off completely. I am a spontaneous, person and patience is not one of my virtues. Me and the Welshman had decided to take a few days R and R at the beach. I occasionally, checked on this ridiculously annoying DNA test. To say I was pissed off was an understatement, and the Welshman was not making matters any better by continuously asking "any news yet love?" No! 23 days later, my little animated truck arrived at the DNA testing laboratory only for yet another tracing chart to turn up with status of package has arrived! What amazes me is, the facts, most of us have waited all our lives for answers but when the time actually comes, the few weeks, wait is torture.

I was in touching distance of finding out, am I alone? To be honest, the weight was starting to get me down and was affecting my mood. Our short but sweet seaside break was over and we headed home (still no DNA results).

A few days later, I was in rapture, my status had changed and I had started to progress in the Laboratory. Finally, I was on the penultimate line I went to bed, hardly sleeping a wink, knowing tomorrow, all my questions would be answered, and if my long lost academic father had produced another family, my family, my siblings, my blood.

I was never one of those children who gently unwrapped their Christmas presents, in fact, the one thing that winds me up more than anything in the world, is when you give someone a present, and they take ages respectfully trying to save the paper. For future use, my eyes would almost pop out of my head with temper. With my inner voice screaming, "Just sodden open it!" I did say patience is not one of my virtues. However, saying that, I am the type of person who could wait a lifetime to get my own back if I've been wronged. In fact, I believe I would probably have made a good sniper. I could just imagine myself hiding disguised as a bush, waiting for hours or days for my quarry to arrive. I think I once read that Einstein said life/pleasure is all part of relativity with the pleasurable parts appearing to be over in seconds, and the painful parts being drawn out for eternity. Me, waiting for the DNA results was sort of in the middle of both! It took me years to analyse character flaws in myself, and one I identified after many mistakes was the fact I enjoy the chase. I'm a hunter, I love fighting for things.

The end result normally leaves me unfulfilled; you know that anti-climax moment. However, in this instance, I found myself hopeful; the feeling of optimism is not natural to me. This feeling in itself made me feel uneasy, like something was going to go wrong. A few days after returning from our holiday my phone let off a small vibration, glancing down. I noticed the words "DNA results ready", and I thought this is it. This is what you've been waiting for. You're finally going to find out how and why you are here. I've been studying up on centimorgans and had a rough idea how it worked well enough to identify a father or sibling. I was nervous however very eager to see my results first thing I saw was 129 CM my heart sank! I knew this was in the level of some distant cousin. I just put down my phone. A few hours later, out of curiosity. I pulled up my big

16

girl pants and decided to have a good look, and to my shock horror surprise, the person who has shared the 129 CM's with was black! No, it doesn't take Einstein to work out that a black person should and would be related to another black person.

However, in my case this was the very first evidence that I actually was black because my entire family were white. I don't mean a few every single one of them blue eyed blondes the profile picture of a black lady made me realise she had to be related to my father in some way, and that was the first time in my entire life that I've ever been connected to the elusive, Mr Abdul Khalil from Africa. I was elated, first time in my life; I'd ever had a connection. My disappointment at the low centimorgan number had turned into a feeling of pure joy! I sat down for a few hours, thinking about how to compose a message to this lady without coming over too desperate. What I wanted to say really was, "I'm lost, and do you know my dad?" So I sent a polite message saying, "I see we are related, could you please give me any information?". I sat all night looking at my phone, and went to bed full of anticipation. Truthfully, silently I'd called this lady every name under the sun, for what I saw as her ignoring me in my hour of need. Paulette did reply. She was very gracious. She lived in London.

She didn't know didn't know very much about her heritage, and no her grandparents or parents were not from Africa. What???

All the time I was thinking they've got to be from bloody somewhere, especially since she's gone back to great grandparent level. She said she would ask her mother and father about their great grandparents and came back the next day. No sorry no Africans in the family, in other words piss off.

I normally work things out, but this time I really was confused. I decided to ditch this DNA crap and carry on with my life. However, like every spoilt and petulant child, I went back deciding to see if there were any more black faces staring out at me who I was related to. There were quite a few. I also looked at my Ethnic roots. As expected there was some African in me however no Sudanese. I also noticed that I was as much Nigerian as I was Scottish!

Now this really did it for me, because as far as I know we've never had a jock in the family, in fact, it was a family joke that no Scotsman had ever put his bagpipes under any of my grannies table. My mother's father was supposed to be Welsh.

I was showing a tiny bit of Welsh DNA. However, nowhere near as much as the Scottish DNA and how the hell did Danish and Norwegian DNA get in to my cells? All I knew, from what it showed I wasn't half African like I always believed. Resigning myself to the fact that My Heritage DNA was the biggest load of crap on the planet, and I should've wiped my arse with the money because I would've had a better result. I gave up, plus I was embarrassed that I'd forced my daughter to buy me the worst birthday present in history.

Funny thing is, I'm obviously black, but I look like I come from lots of different places in fact when travelling abroad I've been asked if I'm Spanish, Egyptian…. and I could list a few different nationalities I've been mistaken for and I started to wonder. I do look like I'm from lots of different places; my features are quite fine I've got full lips, though lots of women have. I've got slim nose and quite soft European features probably more Brazilian looking if it wasn't for my frizzy hair which is now scraped back into a slick topknot.

I accepted you really, couldn't tell my ethnicity. Many things went around in my mind, but I couldn't make head or tail of it, feeling like little miss nobody from the land of nowhere. I admitted the defeat I bitterly regretted taking the damn DNA test for giving me false hope! The poor Welshman I'm married to had to endure hour after hour of me ranting and raving about how crap These DNA companies are! Unlike my very English cousins, even though I was brought up exactly the same, I've never been slow at voicing my opinions, especially when things are not going my way, I have what you would call a very lively personality. I'm very quick to laugh I'm quick to cry and have a temper like a Torpoint chicken!

Torpoint is the border between Devon and Cornwall, and as far as I know, chickens have never been mentioned in their history? But it's an old Plymothian saying, where it comes from nobody knows, I suppose, once upon a time, some drunken sailor decided to steal a chicken and it retaliated in an angry manner.

But I am opinionated, the family joke, I'm completely devoid of shyness. I'm probably the reason my grandmother had to work double shifts, to send me to a drama school, believing my personality to be more fitting to the stage. I could dance a bit once upon a time, I had a beautiful voice, and to everyone surprise was very good at acting.

However, there was one problem. I couldn't remember my lines no matter how hard I tried. No matter how long I studied, I used every trick in the book and I still forgot my lines thank God I was brilliant at ad-libbing once I took off with one of my stories, and they seem to escalate with hilarious consequences.

That's all well and good if you want to become a comedian, however absolutely no good if I was to become an actress.

So that was the end of my acting career I fell at the first hurdle, my grandmother was not pleased. In fact, she was not pleased at all. My one talent is that I can talk to anyone, anywhere. Over the years I found that people were my biggest interest. Yes I'm nosey. However, I'm extremely curious and generally interested in other people's stories, and will think nothing of sitting down for an hour, and having a good conversation with a tramp. I'm extremely attracted to oddballs and eccentrics. That's led me into having some of the most bizarre friends you could imagine. I remember one party I threw; the guest list consisted of a vicar, a prostitute, a thatcher, a surfer, a ballet dancer and a Belsen concentration camp survivor. None of them knew each other. However, every single one of them had in the past had accidentally run into me. I think I've attracted such a diverse pool of friends, is the fact that I am quite naughty, not in a sexual kind of way I'm more slapstick. I laugh very easily and encourage others to do so it's like I never actually really grew up. It's got me into trouble more times than I can mention, but hey Ho, that's life. There's an old saying in my family, where I go trouble it's not far behind! I suppose I remember my grandmother trying educating me in the social graces, it never worked. In fact, one of her descriptions of my character flaws is that I'd "laugh if the cat's ass was on fire". Yes, laugh at anything or anybody, but I'd pursue to the pits of hell if I saw anybody harming an animal.

My love of animals was evident from a very young age, and after the realisation that I was never going to make it as an actress, the family decided that working with animals would probably be the only thing to keep me out of trouble. In my days, in our final year at school, we actually had career lessons with a career officer who was informed by my grandmother to get me a job working with animals. My interview at the local veterinary surgery was a success, and I was offered a job as a trainee veterinary nurse.

My first day at work was horrific for the simple reason I had to wake up at 6 o'clock in the morning. Me and mornings do not get on, unless it entails lying in bed drinking coffee, chatting on the phone, writing in my diary, planning world domination and how I'm going to spend my 200 million lottery win. I am not a morning person as you can gather. I'd like to tell the story of my successful career working with sick animals. However, it was done and dusted within one day. Yes, I got the sack. I suppose threatening to kill the senior surgeon didn't help. To cut a long story short, I was asked to observe the euthanasia of a perfectly healthy animal. I intervened and pleaded for its life.

I totally lost the plot, and it's safe to say my career working with animals was over. It resulted in me getting the sack, threatened with the police and a poor animal losing its life.

I often think about that poor dog! I'm positive animals can sense a pure spirit in people, and that we should trust them a bit more when choosing friends or potential partners. I remember one night staggering home from the clubs and when I say staggering, I was so drunk I could hardly walk. All I could think about was my bed, plus not being sick. It was three flights of stairs up the block of flats I lived in, to my home, and then another steep staircase to my bedroom. I remember, staggering and kicking my shoes off. I'm dropping my clothes as I stagger into my room, desperate to get into my pit, one last push, and then I was in blissful slumber for the next 12 hours. I can remember lying there in my drunken haze, drifting off. Then, to my horror, realising there was somebody in my bed behind me, and he was big all I can remember, is his hairy leg, touching the back of mine and his Stinking breath! I know in romantic literature, a woman's description of unwanted advances, often describes the man as having foul breath.

But this one really did live up to it, he bloody reeked! And then came the noise as he snuggled into the back of my neck, letting out the occasional grunt. The dirty swine, I was truly mortified.

The only thing I could think of was get out fast, why I decided to turn on my bedside lamp first still evades me to this day! To cut a long story short, I jumped up and snapped the light on to confront my attacker! Only to find Albert staring out of the bed covers with sheepish eyes. No Albert was not an old boyfriend or the local peeping Tom, who had found his way in. Albert was my best friends Great Dane! I found out was so distressed at a drunken argument she had had with her boyfriend, that he'd run off in the middle of the night. Obviously thinking he'd get a warm reception from me, poor Albert was badly mistaken. However, we did become friends again when I sobered up the next day… I often think of poor Albert…

Chapter Two

Not Once, But Twice.

Not only did, the delinquent Shirley produce me "the black baby"18 months later, she did it again. This time a beautiful baby boy was presented to the family. Also of questionable heritage, though he was not black. This little bundle of joy was of Asian Indian/Pakistani descent my baby brother (Mohammed, Abdul Tariq Khalil) AKA, Joe, Joey or Jo-Jo long lost for many years until adulthood.

I briefly remember, the times, I spent with Joe as a child, and from a very early age, it was evident he was my mother's son. Joe had inherited Shirley's wit craftiness and charisma. In fact, Joe was like a little jungle book carbon copy of me. In other words, a ready-made biological partner in crime. On our brief reunions, as always, trouble found us to this day it's confirmed to me that family traits are rock-solid and afflictions like madness actually do run in the family. The similarities between me and Joe actually didn't show themselves completely until adulthood, when he arrived at the age of 26, with my mother on one of her visits from London. This was probably the first time I'd seen Joe since his early teens and my God, what a transformation from the clumsy, gawky looking kid to the nearest thing to an Adonis, the local girls, at Plymouth have ever seen! To me, he was still a little shit.

However, we went on to form a lasting and loving bond. It was very easy to love Joe; in fact, I've never met a person man, woman or child who has not instantly fallen in love with him. Charisma just oozed out of him, and my God didn't he know it.

Like myself and mother he knew exactly how to use his charms, however, under the surface, Joe had inherited mine and mothers bad traits. He was totally ruthless when crossed and will do absolutely anything in his power to screw you up. If you dare to step over the line, a real life, Dorian Gray. God knows where he kept his portrait, and probably hid it from me, more than anyone, knowing it would be the first thing I would attack when crossed myself, the other thing that was evident my recently reunited, long, lost brother, was absolutely bloody loaded with money, and loved my love of him. He was in rapture. Throwing his cash and generosity about to my delight. I was a main target, he spoilt me rotten.

There wasn't a thing I didn't get, if I asked. In my small world I had become instantly famous, and the talk of the town, having such wealthy and handsome out of town big city brother. Joe never followed fashion. To be honest, I think he might of been reading the Three Musketeers because truthfully he wouldn't of looked out of place in 17th Century France. Being half Indian, you really couldn't tell where he was from. However, he had the most beautiful hair I've ever seen on anyone, never mind a man. He decided his hair was far too good to cut off, and grew it halfway down his back looking like it had never been cut. However, he admitted to me that he visited plus paid a fortune at the celebrity hairdresser, Vidal Sassoon every month. Where the Majority of men in the late 70s and 80s dressed in tailored clothing Joe decided on a baggy almost Bell sleeved, white silk shirt, unbuttoned to show off his hairy chest, yuck! But at the time the local girls loved it and were practically banging on my door to be let in for a "cup of tea" was the normal excuse! I remember Joe telling me that in London, you were afraid to even make eye contact the people of Plymouth are naturally friendly open and chatty, Joe was like a kid in a sweet shop and was in rapture because of his popularity.

He was treated like a rock star where ever he went in my tiny world. In fact, I believe in all the years that followed I had never seen him happier. I was also happy because his entrance into my life meant that feeling of being alone had disappeared. However, I remember many nights after the parties are finished and the masks were removed, sitting for hours listening to the ranting and raving of a little boy who was abandoned and unloved by his mother. I could take or leave our mother, put it at the back of my mind and shrug off any feelings of resentment, but not Joe. I believe he was traumatised to the extent of what we now recognise as post traumatic shock syndrome. Because, unlike me, Joe was thrown unceremoniously into the care system. Yes, mother dearest had done it again.

Kids just cramped her style. We were an inconvenience when we stop being a weapon to control our fathers. I had an easy upbringing being left in the West Country with a massive loving family, unlike Joe. My grandmother did offer to take in Joe as well and bring us up together. However, mother was not going to have that, saying that I had been completely assimilated by the family which she resented, telling my grandmother that she was not going to have another one turned against her like that spoilt little bitch has, meaning me. This is all because I didn't run into her arms the minute she turned up. But in truth, I was a child, and didn't even know this woman. Remember what I said about the family trait? I didn't love her completely so I was off the team. She cut my brother off out of spite as she didn't want him, but she didn't want anybody else to have him. Because of that, Joe spent his whole childhood in care. Inside, I knew he was messed up, outside to other people he had everything. To strip it down totally naked, to the raw core of feelings he was just my baby brother and I loved him.

Chapter Three

Abracadabra

Everything seemed to get better once Joe is back on the scene, the summer was hotter than normal, and Joe absolutely relished the tradition of my area, of skinny dipping. People say that the folk of Devonport possess no shyness, probably due to the fact that each and every one of us even though well into our 20s 30s 40s 50s, and over, had seen each other naked since the day we could practically walk.

We lived on the water, we lived for the water, and we lived off the water. Many of us were employed due to the water. The only thing we couldn't do was drink the water. However, the only thing that seemed to worry, Joe about getting naked in front of others, was getting out of the water especially in front of the girls, the thought of having a shrunken tiny little dick because of the ice cold water, nothing else. Shopping took on a whole new dimension for me. We were like many low income families, we were used to watching the pennies. Most of my shopping was for food, and pretty things were few and far between. However, with my wealthy and extremely carefree brother shopping for luxuries became an enjoyable pastime. It was more of a sport for my Joe, in fact I'd only have to mention that's nice, or "that's pretty" and he would unceremoniously pop the items into the shopping basket, with not a care in the world about the cost. Jesus I was loving every single minute of it, one his jumpers alone cost more than a month's rent for me; he was so bloody extravagant, something that never left him.

Even when he was skint himself Joe just didn't know how to budget. Sorry I'll correct that he didn't want to budget. He didn't like cheap things, and would rather go naked then wear market gear, or mass-produced rubbish, as he used to say. Christmas became magical again, with Joe deciding he needed to be with the family for Christmas day no matter how late on Christmas. Regardless of the weather, or time of day, he would make that journey from London to Plymouth. Grabbing any present, in any service station, regardless of cost. The magic of sitting around a family dinner table on Christmas Day was new to Joe, and he enjoyed every single minute of it. He enjoyed being part of a family, the laughter, even the arguments, after we'd all had too much to drink. He loved the snacks, the open fire, and the ridiculously old-fashioned reruns of Morecambe and Wise on the television.

It was all that Joe had dreamed of. Many years later, I remember sitting looking out of the window waiting for my wayward brother to arrive on yet another freezing Christmas Eve. I realised that I'd listen to one song on every Christmas Eve when waiting for Joe to arrive. Chris Rea's "Driving home for Christmas!" Only last year, did I actually listen to the words, especially the lyrics that describe, driving home for Christmas, driving home to (hallowed ground). The first Christmas that I heard this song after Joe had left us, I howled not only for his loss, but also for everyone's loss who loved him. Most of all, I felt sorry and still do feel sorry for myself. I understand grief can take a long time to get over. However, part of me actually doesn't want to get over it. Why should I? It's my grief, as far as I'm concerned, it's absolutely nothing to do with anyone else. I feel "getting over it" as they say, is like letting go, and I'm far from ready to let go, I can assure you.

I more than most suffered and paid a heavy price, mentally physically and emotionally due to the demise of my brother, so why should I let go, just like that?

In fact, "paying a price", is a damn understatement of what I went through, and subsequently what my family went through having to deal with, and the aftershock of what happened to me brought, on by the death of Joe. His cancer almost took the both of us, thankfully, little bit of me was saved. I say thankfully, sometimes the ungrateful side of me doesn't accept that statement, I'll finish here before I start wallowing in self-pity, something that I despise.

I'll just yank up my big girl pants, and crack on, like I have always done to cope with adversity and trauma that enters my life. Deal with it the Devonport way and the only way I know how.

Robinson Crusoe the loss
Poem.
By Lizzie Khalil. © 2024

Anyone who has suffered loss will understand the feeling of being completely isolated and alone. Just like being stranded on a desert island, you may find food, water and shelter. However, you are still stranded and completely on your own…

You find yourself going around in circles, constantly looking for a way out, constantly looking for that ship in the distance. Praying to be found, praying for your nightmare to be over. You light warning fires, for passing ships to see, using any tool no matter how crude to write out that desperate,

"Please help", a message searching for a Man Friday to alleviate your solitude and pain.

Loneliness and isolation become a fight for survival, but you continue to be on your own, something none of us have prepared for. Something each and every one of us will hopefully experience at least one point in our lives, because without the pain it means you have never loved or been loved.

You feel like a fish, trying to swim in syrup you feel everything and nothing at the same time, nothing is logical and absolutely nothing makes sense.

(Lizzie Khalil). 2024

Unlike most people, I developed these feelings long before we parted. I became resentful that the little shit had the audacity to just up and die leaving me alone. Analysing it many years later, I realised I was mourning for myself. Joe had a saying about selfish people like me, and would say over and over, "it's all me, me, me, me, me!"

Technically he was right, because apparently, he had gone to a "better place" Heaven if you are Christian, basking in eternal peace of the lord. Or marrying   virgins.

Me? I'd prefer the Viking pagan alternative to any kind of Heaven. "Valhalla" is where you find yourself entering a massive fire lit drinking hall, filled with all your old friends and do nothing but eat, drink, and then party for eternity!

Throw in a few good old fights and yes, that would be heaven for me I think being in eternal peace would bore the shit out of me. No, thanks!

Chapter Four

Blanche

Talking about peace, reminds me of my grandmother. There is a long story behind the name. Grannies name was, Blanche Victory Peace, she was a fisherman's daughter. As I previously said, Blanche had a hard beginning; I think it must be something about her generation because they wore hardship. They seemingly enjoyed the trials and tribulations their class faced. They suffered like it was something they were expected to do. They were poor from the bottom of the food chain and rather than wallow in their misfortune, they challenged the hardship with the belief that hard work and perseverance would prevail.

Surprisingly, in many cases it did. One of her fondest memories as a child was one of being given a roast potato, in payment for running an errand for a more well off neighbour. I can't imagine the youth of today, or even myself, or my generation, being grateful for a soddin' roast potato? But there you go, that's how they perceived life. Work, do the job, because any payment was worthwhile in the end, and as I said her life was hard. Truthfully only now I've come to realise just how much I admired her. Years ago, when I was younger, I resented her for being a pushover. I remember once calling her a bloody doormat for letting other people walk all over her, I now I see it as her strength, a stoicism that mine or our younger generation and all the spoilt, entitled brats walking around would know absolutely nothing about.

She also liked to plan, and refused point blank to receive any form of what she called charity. From an early age, she drummed it into me, pontificating, "Pay your rent ", then you can starve in private, pay your way, and owe nobody nothing! And do not go cap in hand to anyone, because once you do "they've" got you", who they were I do not know? Probably the upper classes, I suppose.

She spent most of her working life as a cleaner for "those rich people" and took enormous pride in her work. She would go above and beyond the call of duty to see every element of her work was in tip top condition, and believe me; her efforts were not ignored by the so-called rich people. I remember one occasion, when my poor Gran broke her arm. On this occasion, the old bugger got no sympathy for me! Harsh, but read on. I remember her looking up to me with tears in her eyes holding the offended appendage looking for sympathy. No need, because on this occasion she wasn't going bloody to get it. It was a, "it's your own fault gran from me," yes, I know that sounds harsh, but this time I had to be cruel to be kind in truth, she was very lucky it was 1987", the year of the great storm that hit the UK. It caused a massive amount of damage, death and destruction throughout the country. It was by immortalised the BBC's famous weatherman, Michael Fish, who answered a call from a very worried lady on live TV. She asked are we going to be hit with the hurricane that was raging across the Atlantic, after it had dealt with our American cousins? I remember the "I am a God" weatherman, Michael Fish, looking right into the camera, smiling and patronising down the phone, with an "of course not dear" the worst of it is going to miss us completely!

And guess what? the UK was literally torn to pieces bit by bit over the next 24-hour period, nothing frightens me especially where the elements are concerned living on the coast I've come to love storms.

However, on this occasion I was genuinely shitting myself. I can remember sitting on my bed with a feeling of pressure behind my eyes, and ringing in my ears. It was such a strange feeling that something bad was going to happen, and going to happen fast! That was the first and last time I'd ever felt like that. The feeling rose into a crescendo of buzzing sounds, at that moment I generally felt pure blind panic. When all of a sudden three of my bedroom windows spontaneously exploded, filling the room with the most tremendous storm I've ever experienced. Glass was swirling around, shredding anything in its path including me, it was like the horror movie Poltergeist! and not something I'd like to experience again.

But let's get back to my poor old Gran and her broken wing. She's not getting off that easy. As I've explained, The Messiah of the weathermen, Michael Fish prediction was utterly and totally wrong. The country was battered, and people were genuinely losing cars, their businesses, and their property and in some case their lives! On strict orders from me, granny Blanche was ordered to stay indoors and away from all windows. I remember the challenge of trying to get to the corner shop that day. I was ducking and diving to avoid the multitude of flying obstacles, just to buy my Grans bloody fags, plus her four tins of Mackeson stout that she couldn't live without. For back up, I took Brian, a friend with me. Realistically, it was more for the company because Brian was at the bottom of the food chain when God handed out masculinity, there was very little he could do in the way of physical support.

I used him more of a mascot that day I suppose. First thing I remember was his legs slowly, rising off the ground; he was hanging onto a lamppost for dear life at the time. The wind was that strong! However, me being a fat bugger all my life had paid off, providing me with a lot more ballast. I suppose you could call it a lucky fat anchor. Seeing his legs rising off the ground up to the air, all I could think of was Dorothy from the Wizard of Oz. Years later, Brian went on to have more similarities to Dorothy and her red shoes then just flying up into the air, but that's another story!

Granny Blanche was the most grateful person I've ever seen that day. She was terrified she was going to be without her beloved fags and booze for the whole day she praised us to the hilt for our courage and fortitude. Me and Brian had made it back eventually. However, we experienced A Close Encounter of the Third Kind, an actual alien mothership, just like the one from Steven Spielberg's, famous film, when it hovered above our heads. I quickly thought of warning Brian to prepare himself to be probed by the aliens however, I do remember thinking he would have probably enjoyed it. Only to find out later, it was the entire roof of one of the dockyards South yard boat hangers. And trust me; these things were big, big enough to house a battleship.

The storm was that bad. Like all British people in times of adversity that First thing we did was to put the kettle on! Me and my companion had survived and Gran had her booze and precious fags. All we had to do now, was ride out this bloody devil of a storm. The power station had gone down. Thank God in those days, we relied on an open fire and a gas cooker so we were not going to freeze, or starve we just needed to entertain ourselves until the storm passed. It had died down a little bit in the last few hours to what I will call now a bad storm. It looked like the hurricane had finally passed. Thankfully, however you still wouldn't want to venture out in it if you valued your life! I was enjoying the fact I could now tell the story of "how I battled the great storm of 1987, and survived!

However, Granny Blanche almost didn't. She would often tell stories of how the Luftwaffe and the German bombs did not stop her from doing anything she wanted to do. Boasting how she would dodge the might of the German air force, why? Just because she wanted to, adding "the bloody Germans didn't frighten me! Then going into her Hitler kiss my ass routine!

But my darling Gran went behind my back after I'd battled a hurricane in order to keep her fags and drink, plus almost losing Brian up a vortex. I did this because I believed if I did let her go on her own outside that day, I would probably never see her again, she was that bloody tiny, there was a strong possibility she could have been picked up and carried by the wind, not seen again until she landed up the line, probably in Dorset!

However, unbeknown to me at the time, the sly old bugger had used us for her own ends, we'd been stitched up like a kipper, because all the time she had been secretly planning to sneak up to her beloved social club! The Ker Street social club to give it its correct title was like a bloody magnet to her. I can't count the amount of times that I've received a call with the message, "Elizabeth please come and get your Gran she's drunk!" The next day she'd always start denying the fact, using the same old excuse time after time that she must have eaten something that was off, and was in fact not drunk but delirious with food poisoning! She insisted it was the idiotic bar staff who had mistaken her case of poisoning as drunkenness.

Yes, I've heard it all before Gran lol. However, on the day of the great storm, only a couple of diehards even dared to venture out to the Kerr Street Social Club. Apparently, she'd only managed to sink two "Maccy D" stouts before she was told they were closing up for the day   for some reason she point blank refused the offer from the bar staff to ring me, in order to help her home. By now we "all know why".

 Apparently one witness who was looking out of his front room, window said that my pocket sized Gran was unceremoniously picked up by the storm and carried about 15 feet on the wind and slammed at the bottom of fifteen concrete steps! He also went on to describe her having her legs practically wrapped around her neck with her knickers in the air! (She would have hated that bit most of all lol) She was so lucky that day, thankfully a couple of strong lads gave her a Fireman's lift back to her house, they did their best to and managed to fashion a sling out of an old tea towel even asking the next door neighbour who her family were, and if they had a phone number? You see they put the reason down to shock. Why? The old lady had point blank refused to give them a contact phone number for her family, once again we all know why!

They demanded her family would want be informed of her dice with death! She had no option but to give in to their demands and painfully gave up my phone number...

I couldn't bloody believe it when I got the call especially when they described her being in a bad way! I was seething! I truthfully could have killed her. The sly old sod had gone too far this time! Not only did I (quickly evaluate my life) have delinquent kids, a drunken delinquent mother, I now had living proof of a crafty, delinquent bloody old grandmother as well!

As we say in the West Country, she really was an old bugger. However, her antics have given me years of laughter and hundreds of humorous stories to pass on to my children. Even though she didn't have a funny bone in her body, and she couldn't tell a joke to save her life, it was the situations she got herself into; many of them with hilarious outcomes that live on to this day, meaning her sins and her many misdemeanours were always forgiven by those who loved her, and especially me.

Chapter Five

The Breakup

I always knew I was different. Not only because I looked so different, than every other single member of have my family, friends or people in my environment, but the difference I had felt come from deep inside. Probably down to genetics, or the fact I was an arrogant sod who always wanted a bit more. Who always had to walk the extra step to see what's around the corner, to always look up when others around me were looking down. As I got older, I realised I'm just a bit odd, more flattering acquaintances describe me as unique. Gran used to say they broke the mould when they made my Elizabeth, not always said as a term of endearment.

I found school boring, and was often chastised for looking out of the windows. Daydreaming, I suppose of what, I had no idea. I suppose I'm just a bit of a dreamer as I've previously mentioned, ordinary people are of no interest to me. I seem to be highly attracted to oddities or people with strange ways. I've always found people with criminal tendencies, interesting. I admire people who took the chance to better their lives with a non-violent criminality, such as the Walter Mitty character faking his own death for the insurance money. Even though I'm far too old to enjoy rap music, I identify with Eminem's lyrics "One Shot". It's my favourite song, the words, about if you had one chance to change your life, would you take it? Hell, yes! As long as the crime is against big corporations, who cares if the fat cat CEO is robbed of a few pounds? Truthfully, they probably wouldn't even notice, I'd say definitely not, and in a lot of cases they are equally as guilty of a few misdemeanours themselves.

Blanche was very honest, and as far as I know, had never broken a law, criminal or moral in her life she's very often quoted as saying, "thieves deserve to have their fingers chopped off". However, often stated she would rather have a thief than a liar. Her explanation was, you can catch a thief a lot easier than a liar! Her righteous beliefs, in being honest at all costs, lead her to being ripped off and the victim of deception more times than she'd had hot dinners. One way to describe her was a trusting fool, in the belief, if you were clean and well-spoken the chances of you being a bad egg were very low indeed, where the dirty unemployed or homeless were not to be trusted.

Chapter Six

Beauty Tips

One thing Gran did was to install in me was to look after myself. Make sure you looked your best at all times and I quote, "you never know who you might meet?

"She took great care of her appearance, and, despised any woman who didn't make the most of the assets God had given them. From a very early age, she saved regularly to buy the latest fashion items, and she loved and adored Hollywood movie stars. It was the glamour that enticed her like a moth to a candle. This resulted in my mother, the delinquent Shirley Rose, being named after grans favourite child actress the very talented, but probably exploited Shirley Temple.

My mother was a beautiful child. However, she possessed absolutely zero talent when it came to singing, dancing or performing in anyway. When I was born Gran quickly took charge. Naming me, Elizabeth, named after the very beautiful, and many times married Elizabeth Taylor. This time she got it almost right, as I did go on to resemble the beautiful Miss Taylor. Probably because of the amount of husbands I've acquired over the years, plus apparently she enjoyed a drink or two in a few of her films.

I also inherited the adoration of glamour, and to this day I do believe I'm more flamboyant than most women, especially at the age I am now. In fact, I recently read an article stating how middle-aged British women, especially British middle-aged women feel invisible. To be brutally honest, looking at some of them, invisibility probably would be a blessing. As I previously stated I'm a people person. I observe, I'm nosey, and people watching is a hobby of mine. I'm one of these people could sit on a park bench for hours with no newspapers or books needing no one to talk to, I just like to sit and watch, one of the things I have observed is the uniform, or I should say more like a bloody cult of middle-aged women, who, for some reason believe once they reach a certain age, they feel the need to look like men! Because if I saw one, I saw 100 on my last visit out people watching practically 99% of them had cropped, grey, short back and sides haircuts. Tracky bottoms, and a fleece jacket, with no make up to be seen. It wouldn't surprise me if half of them were wearing men's boxer shorts as well. They look like a brigade of old men most of them!

The majority of them were being followed by downtrodden husbands; to be honest the majority look like they have given up the will to live. Truthfully looking at the women they married, I don't bloody blame them.

One thing Granny Blanche never did was to give up on her appearance. To the very last she demanded her hair dye; I remember her saying, why would any woman want to look bloody old? She despised grey hair, saying not even older gay men want to sleep with a little old grey man, and it's no wonder that men's eyes start wondering when their wives start resembling one! I suppose by now, the readers mental picture of my physical appearance is starting to build, I probably could have been the complete package apart from the fact of my lifelong weight problem. Gran used to say that I've got big bones! Well that's her excuse and I'm sticking to it.

However I do like the finer things of life. The top of my list being food, I don't mean just any old food. In fact if I had to just eat food just to keep me alive I will probably be anorexic by now. I got fat on the very best money could buy, and have spent a lifetime consuming the very best Mother Nature could provide. I managed that feat by consuming mostly meat, fish and vegetables, throw in healthy, grains and pulses and that's been my lifelong diet. Yes, eating too much of it as made me a fat knacker over the years.

However, my looks for my age is a testament to eating well, because I look years younger than most women my age who are mostly wrinkled old ladies. I know, I look in the mirror wondering when it's going to be my turn, but so far, my complexion is still youthful. My eyes are still bright, and my hair is still luscious and smooth. I can't put it all down to nutrition because I do spend quite a lot of time in maintenance. However, it's paid off because the Welshman who is quite a bit younger than me still fancies the pants of me, he tries to hide it but he forgets he's dealing with an expert, and that I've had years of experience in reading men.

Once I get a whiff of interest from a man, that's it, the poor sod, is a goner. Over the years, I realised it's absolutely unimportant for a woman to be good in bed. What is important is that a man thinks a certain woman is going to be good between the sheets, and that's the key to keep them guessing. I believe 99% of sexual attraction is in the brain, women need to be their man's fantasy. Because, come on girls when he's thinking, I bet you he's not thinking about anybody else is he? It's a well-known fact that those men will never marry the girl who drops her knickers, at the first wink of an eye. How a woman could possibly be flattered being pursued by a species who have been known to shag anything when desperate enough!

Living in the naval town I've heard it all, especially the debauchery men are capable of. You hear the jokes about wanking into a sock, about them poking that adolescent dick in the hole in their mattress, horror stories of mortuary attendants getting there sick kicks molesting corpses. And Jesus Christ I remember a story of a young sailor who took a ship mate home for the holidays and the ungrateful sod repaid the families hospitality by shaggin' the Christmas turkey the night before Christmas! Thankfully, the poor thing was well dead by that point, and the six-hour cooking time destroyed, any harmful bacteria, (we hope) Men, gross, not all but an awful lot of them!

I suppose we could judge vileness and sickness on a sliding scale from innocent to obscene, and then we have the protectiveness of the mother, my Gran. She was overprotective, most of my life. In her own words, she freely admitted this, and one of her sayings is, I watch my Elizabeth, like a hawk. She hated me playing out on my own, and kept a firm hold on my whereabouts unlike the rest of the kids in my street. I felt absolutely trapped by this old woman, who should I say was only in her 40s when she became a grandmother for the first time. I do believe this is where my deceitfulness stems from, because I always had to lie if I ever wanted to do anything other than what she told me to do. To be honest, I hated her for it. I just couldn't understand why once again I was singled out, making me even more detached from my peer group. You know as if being black and fat wasn't bad enough to make me stand out.

I had to be overprotected by a dragon, most of the time. She never ever trusted men she liked them well enough, but she never trusted them, especially where children were concerned. She once told me there's something inside of a man and thankfully, with good upbringing and schooling, what's inside hopefully stays inside she had six sisters. None of them were like this to my knowledge. However, they all shared a family secret. A family secret that was so horrific, even they could not discuss it with each other. As I said previously, she loved a drink; she was never much of a spirit person. It was always the ale, specifically stout which is a very dark heavy alcoholic version of beer.

She used to say it's a food source all on its own. However, the government and the NHS at the time promoted this ideology because anybody who has ever given blood will remember in the good old days. After they'd drained you of the required amount, which was 1 pint of the good stuff from your veins, you were rewarded with half a pint of Guinness. Apparently, it's rich in iron and helps to top up the red blood cells. Plus, it was the only alcoholic drink allowed on a maternity ward to help in the recovery of new mothers. My mother, the delinquent Shirley Rose was a complete disciple of this practice, and is probably the only person I've ever known to become an alcoholic purely for medicinal purposes, her recovery from my birth lasted until her death, which was about 35 years

I must admit, one of the nicest alcoholic drinks I've ever experience was a drink called a velvet stout, my God, that beverage literally slips down your throat. I can well understand how one could become addicted to that creamy rich alcoholic beverage, so I stayed well away!

This was probably a good thing, considering that neither my grandmother nor my mother had a weight problem, unlike me, If I had followed their example, God knows what state I would've been in. I would've probably ended up one of these people where the Fire Brigade were called to oversee the craning out of a morbidly obese person who had been bedbound for years, no, I'm glad I left the stout alone. After one of her sessions my Gran always became responsive to questions. She used to say I've got to be careful when I'm drunk, because my Elizabeth pumps me for information.

That was the very best time, sometimes encouraged by me to have just one more drink Gran and then we'll go home. That's when I gained any information I needed. At this point, I'd completely given up asking questions about my father because no matter how drunk how out of it or delirious she was the only information I could get was he was a black African man! One occasion I remember information was offered to me freely which came as a bit of a surprise. Considering the fact, she was always guarded and was secretive by nature. On this occasion, she started to talk about her youth and how she was molested, or should I say they attempted to molest my grandmother. The perpetrators being two soldiers. Unwelcome advances, that she encountered on her way back from the chip shop one night. I tried to make a joke about the fact that they were probably after the fish and chips more than her. That made me laugh but it threw her into a rage. Aiming her attack at all men in general, she started to call them dirty sods, ranting, that dirty swine's needed to be strung up or thrown into the river with a large stone around their necks.

At this point, I could see her mood was getting very dark. Which was uncommon for my grandmother's tantrums, or screaming tantrums. Should I say were common when she lost her temper in drink, but not this dark, and definitely not morbid, like she had become that night. She started muttering under her breath, about what she'd do, if she ever got her

45

hands on the dirty rotten swine's. That she would probably tear his sodden throat out, all the time there's me thinking what the hell has she not told me? When the truth finally came out. I was filled with great sadness and pity for one of the gentlest creatures; I've ever met in my life. My Aunt Betty, whose real name was Malvina, every single female in the family related or not had the title auntie in front of their name to us kids. Looking back, Betty was one of us kids. Yes, she was years older, however, mentally she was just a child. A very young child at that. She was severely disabled, with a crooked spine that made her limp on one side, she had a dominant leg, and her other leg seem to fly out and propel her along. It's hard to describe a physical disability, unless you're describing something like blindness or deafness, which can be defined.

Poor old Betty was just crooked and I'll leave it at that. She was never able to lead a normal life and was taken care of and lived with Blanche's older sister Mariah, (Ria) who was like the rock of the family. She a was funny, no nonsense, feisty woman who didn't bother with her hair or make up and would mess you up if you dared to cross her, or all my auntie's. I loved Ria more than any of them! Like a lot of the children in the family if we had a problem, especially as teenagers, best thing to do was just rock up to her house. You got fed, watered, and your ass kicked and told to "buck up" and get the hell over yourself.

She believed in tough love. An example I have followed because I do believe you can make matters far worse by wallowing in it. Old school, my aunt Ria. Apparently, she had been caring for Betty all her adult life. The only alternative was an institution after my great grandmother's death. Apparently the family were thrown into chaos on the death of my great grandma with the decision of what to do with the severely mentally, and physically disabled Betty, I always believed or assumed, should I say that Betty was a victim of spina bifida, until I got older, realising that spina bifida victims were not necessarily mentally impaired such as my aunt Bet, horrible to think how some of us draw short straws In life.

When the full story was revealed rather than anger, because that came later, I was hit with an overpowering sadness. All those years of bitterness and ranting and raving, from my grandmother, Blanche was justified, because of what had happened to my poor aunt Betty. It is even too painful for me to talk about even now. However, I'm telling the story so I just as well get on with it. To dress up, or dramatize it just because I'm writing this book seems obscene, so I'm going to tear it down to the basics.

When little Betty was five years old she was enticed away from her older siblings by a man who to this day is unknown. The family searched for Betty. From what I've been told my frantic family searched for about five hours without success, until they could hear a high-pitched whistling, which turned out to be the whistle of a policeman, something they carried as part of their uniform.

The policeman who had been alerted to the disappearance of our Betty had searched the local train lines and ponds, apparently there he found what he thought was the body of a small child; tragically hit by a train it turned out to be our Betty.

Her poor little body, broken, battered bruised and bleeding at the side of the railway track, many years later, when describing this horrible scenario, my Gran described the panic and hysterics, especially from her mother, my great grandmother, Elizabeth Hill. She ran flat out up the wet street, screaming my baby is dead. This was a feat in its self for my great grandmother, as she was an extremely large woman who could obviously move when she wanted to.

The equivalent of our emergency services in those days got to work in recovering the body of little Betty. The description of the weather that day was, raining cats and dogs! Overcast and miserable, to be honest regarding the scenario that description is an understatement if there ever was one, apparently it was three hours past the time when they first heard the police man's whistle when the emergency services began the removal of Betty Hills body, they were obviously not in too much of a rush Plus even in those days evidence still need to be collected, then according to Blanche absolute pandemonium broke loose from what she described as screams from the men in attendance, because as we know years ago that would've been classed as men's work! Women being far too delicate to deal with highly stressful situations like this, so the sound of a great big tough man screaming really did set the alarm bells ringing!

Against all the odds, our Bet was alive barely breathing, but life was still in that tiny battered body. All Gran remembered at this time was seeing her mother Lizzie tearing there two up two down tiny dwelling to pieces, grabbing any bit of bedding she could get her hands on at the time, screaming over and over again, cover her up for God's sake cover my baby up please keep her dry.

This incident traumatised my grandmother for the rest of her life, and to be perfectly honest after me, witnessing, Blanche's regression into her past, traumatised me as well. After doctors had examined Betty's "train accident" the true horror of the situation was made apparent. No, Betty was not hit by the passing locomotive, I'm not going to dress it up; I'm just going to say it how it was told to me, "some dirty rotten swine" had raped her! Yes, raped a Child, barely five years old, if that wasn't bad enough, the sick twisted twat decided to torture her as well. The result of that torture was the reason for Betty's lifelong disability, I was right to be suspicious about the spina bifida, not being the cause of her disablement.

Because of her torture, Betty received a broken back as part of her ordeal. Thankfully, Betty remembered nothing and spent the next two years learning how to walk again. It was a further two years before she could articulate as Gran described. Her sister has been struck dumb with the shock.

The perpetrator was never caught, which led my grandmother to become suspicious of every single man in her environment, the ordinary people of the Barbican Plymouth believed rightly, or wrongly it had to have been an outsider considering the fact the port was filled daily with foreign fishermen, however, he could've been there next door their next door neighbour. It could've been a family friend. Gran believes this is more likely, because Betty was a clingy and shy child and would not have "gone off" with a stranger. Malvina Hill, grew into adult hood, oblivious to any facts, because of her ordeal the whole family made sure that she was now always safe and happy.

From what I recall, Betty was extremely happy most of the time like a child she enjoyed attention, outings and most of all sweeties resulting in a chubbiness that suited her. I remember her almost knocking myself and my small cousins off our feet to be the first recipient of the cakes and ice cream that followed our massive family. Sunday dinners, a child's mind, yes however, she weighed about 10 stone heavier than any of us kids! The families understanding was to just keep an eye on her knowing she was inadvertently a danger because she had the mind of a child, and boisterousness of a kid. The story was put to bed, regardless of her ordeal, she outlived practically all of them and I found out too late, that Betty did eventually end up in the institution that the family had worked so long and so hard to keep her out of.

50 years later and a completely different generation, I found myself on the cusp of identifying her attacker! Completely by accident, I was no Sherlock Holmes and was not obsessed with solving a family mystery. Revelations arose, completely incidental and by accident when I was in conversation with a very old lady, who was a grandmother of an acquaintance of mine. We hear descriptions such a "spine chilling" or the hair stood up on the back of my neck. I'll add another one to that because every bit of colour drained from my face, yes, my black African face to boot! Because I went white when I heard this revelation, leading me to believe, and trust, that (old wives' stories) are there to guide and warn us when other things make no sense.

Chapter Seven

The New King

Devonport's new king arrived out of nowhere, a bit like the destroyers in the war of the worlds. They had always been here hiding lying dormant waiting for their time to strike; we just never noticed them before. However, when Nathan Picket announced his arrival, it was with all the impact and fanfare of a real life king, surrounded by hordes of servants, and people more than willing to do his bidding. He was wealthy, adored and pandered to by his people, or should I say, the minions in his court. To the antimonarchist on the other side of the coin, Picket was a dangerous bully; he was a total asshole who had managed to corner the market in narcotics.

The local youth had started to dabble with hard drugs about 12 months before, in my reckoning. However, pot and amphetamine based drugs had been around for donkeys years Long gone, and frowned on were the opium dens. No, Nathan Pickets drugs were trendy, young, different little tablets with cool designs and smiley faces printed or embossed, whose sole purpose was to keep you up all night, raving mad, along with the multitudes of downers needed to slow the brain down, enabling you to sleep at after you'd been up all night and sometimes days.

In fact, Nathan was the talk of the town. He became sort of a rock star to his customers, the sort of person the likes of me would never know or understand. They'd say the older people of Devonport, I was 28 at the time, one of the parents, and was positively to be kept out of the drugs loop because we identified as some kind of threat. A grass, the most detested bottom dweller of a council estate.

The people who would drop you into the police at a moment's notice, and with that Nathan started his reign of terror, not that he was a hard man or superior street fighter. The detestable Nathan had his minions the dirty tricks brigade, young boys in his power who would venture out in the dead of night and put a brick for your grannies window or dump inflammables through your letterbox when you were asleep at night, burning your home down and your children to death.

This was not the Devonport I knew where conflicts were sorted with a good argument sometimes a good old fist fight, one of many of Devonport's honest conflict resolutions. This was something else. This was cowardly, sly and worst of all, his henchman were nothing more than children or mentally inadequate druggies, to be perfectly honest. We were for the first time afraid because they worked in the dark, they lied. They had no courage and were impossible to catch. The worst bit about it, they were our children who were being controlled by this revolting Pied Piper.

Something had to be done. Mr Richardson who was left alone by the rest of us, for one simple reason that being Mr Richardson was a goody two shoes. Who would think nothing of calling the council over a misplaced dustbin or an overturned park bench.

He often called the police and complained constantly over such minor inconveniences. He was like the boy who cried wolf. The police never took any notice of him whatsoever at this point. We'd wished we had not taken the piss out of him so much in the past because if we ever needed a grass, it was now! To cut a long story short Mr Richardson phoned the police complaining about the undesirables running, rough shot in our back alleys in total about 50 times. All his complaints were carefully logged in his diary and like the boy who cried wolf he was ignored. But something had to be done about Nathan Picket, and it had to be done fast, but what? When you add drink to any conversation in Devonport, you get one of two outcomes, immense joy and slapstick, comedy or hell, fire damnation, unfortunately, there is no in between I'm afraid with the Devonportothens "WE SHOULD KILL THE BASTARD! "

And that was it, it was decided and for some reason I knew this was coming. Thinking about it so did everybody else. However, 1, who was going to be the 1st to say it. 2, how were we going to do it? And Last but not least when? In truth none of this was important, having witnessed the extent of how Devonport people react and drink, I knew this was all talk venting and ranting and raving was part of their bravado. This was just the Devonport Way; very rarely did anybody ever follow up on the threat. It was just like virtual retribution they just liked to get it off their chests. However deep inside I longed for this revolting individual to be gone and to say I hate him was an understatement looking back I realised I probably never hated anybody up to that point as much as I hated Nathan Picket.

This hatred, or should I say "intense hatred" developed on the only occasion I had interaction with him personally. It was a Saturday afternoon and I was having a cup of tea and a good old gossip with my friend Brian, the one who almost got sucked up into the vortex in the storm. As usual, we talked shit, that's the terminology for chitchat in Devonport. Another word talking about meaningless things very often funny but of no importance. Suddenly the hair went up on the back of my neck, call it female intuition, but I could feel it, and jumped up looking out of my kitchen window. Then I heard it the cry of my little girl, Tamsin she was a loud child and often exaggerated. However, this time I could see by the bright red face that she was deadly serious. I knew something bad had happened. I think I cleared the three flights of stairs in less than 20 seconds taking two steps at a time, I was grossly overweight, but Jesus I could move when I wanted to. I met her at the bottom of the stairs I remember shaking her to tell me "What has happened?" No cuddles that would come later.

I needed the information and I needed it now! "He, he, and they" she blurted it out. "A, a, a, a man is going to kill Lucky!" She was absolutely sobbing! And grabbed my hand. I can't tell you how long it took us to get to the top of our road, but it was pretty fast. I was greeted with poor Lucky who was the gentlest little dog in the world, hunched on the floor, cowering at the feet of yes, that swine Nathan Picket! I think I explained earlier on in my story my intense love of animals, any animal, especially mine! By this time, Nathan Picket had been bragging. He'd purchased a gun, just in case any of "them" meaning Davenport people got out of hand.

I remember dropping Tamsin's hand and barking the order stay there! I can also remember moving my 19 stone bulk at full-pelt in order to get to my little dog! I remember Picket was holding what I now know to be a baseball bat in his hand, probably to look even more menacing.

But I was blind, completely utterly blind. I was acting on instinct and as far as I was concerned, not even God himself would get that dog off me no chance, I had swept Lucky up into my arms. She was under my protection now and what will be will be I thought it was a stand-off now, (I WAS NOT GOING TO BACK DOWN) Personally, I should have been shitting myself, but apparently adrenaline is a powerful substance, stronger than any drug. Followed by something a coward like him would never understand, and that's courage something any bully would never possess, it's the one thing a bully is the most terrified of! I swear to this day, I could actually hear Brian's heart beating outside of his chest, and that's when it happened!

I could see confusion in the bullying bastard's eyes. One thing I pride myself on is being able to read people and predict accurately the outcomes of a situation and in that split second, I saw fear not of a physical threat, but The fear of not knowing what to do in his eyes.

His face turned grey as a colour drained from it, it was in that split second, I decided to go for it! Before he had time to think the bastard was off guard, and I knew it, if I'd given him the chance to think he would've had no choice, but to save face, and probably shoot us dog and all or batter the living daylights of us in order to set an example to the rest of our community, and that was it, I unleashed Hell, in good old fashion Devonport style, all topped up with my African hot blood. From what I've seen, it's a brave or very stupid man who picks a fight with a mother especially one born and raised in Devonport!

Poor old Lucky the dog, for her own protection was slung unceremoniously onto the grass verge, with my arms open wide and my gigantic tits swinging in the wind, I screamed at the top of my voice, well come on if you're gonna do it, do it now twat! He started to take one step towards me. Suddenly, Brian was in between the both of us, to this day I don't remember his actual input, but lo and behold Nathan backed off to the disbelief of his gang, who, by this time looked terrified. In typical Lizzie style, me never doing anything by halves, I thought well I've come this far I'll just as well go to the whole bloody hog and I started ranting and raving screaming profanities, all the time slapping my fat thigh with my hand I remember stamping my bear feet on the pavement, yes, I'd completely lost the soddin plot, and I didn't give a shit either! Me and Brian had the drug dealing bastard over a barrel, he had to react now or never! No way out. He knew it, I knew it everyone in bloody earshot knew it!

React he did by turning around, calling his minions, screaming twats at us as he legged it back to his den! Personally, I think it was a fact, my hair was sticking up all over the place when I ran at him with no bra on, I must've looked like some kind of deranged, crazed overweight Zulu warrior on crack, looking back at it that scared him most.

Or it could have the fact in the middle of that stand-off he suddenly heard the voice of "Dorothy" you know the wimpiest person on the planet, when he just screamed bloody leave her alone! In truth I was at the time, and still am absolutely sodding gobsmacked with what came out of Dorothy's mouth that day, even more gobsmacked was the look on the new King of Devonport's face? We will never know but unbeknown to us at the time we had entered into the Devonport equivalent of the fight, at the O.k. Corral!

The contenders being Lizzie complete with an unkempt Afro! With her massive tits hanging out! Brian "Dorothy" the wimpiest and most un-confrontational person in the world willing to have a go, drug dealing gangster with a baseball bat and his gun?

Who happened to be nothing more than a big chicken at heart?

All over Lucky the little terrier dog!

Chapter Eight

The King is dead

The thing I've come to realise when we are trying to tell a story, is the story line is not linear you start in one direction then find yourself being diverted to the point you can find yourself going around in bloody circles. Sometimes we find ourselves circling and dwelling on something we'd rather not remember, like the highly unpleasant people we cross paths with. When I say unpleasant, I mean some absolutely rotten bastards we encounter on this journey called life.

As I've said previously, Devonport was a magical place to grow up. Every woman was your auntie, and every man was your uncle. I remember when I was going to the shops and it was auntie this, and uncle that, to everybody I met on my small journey to buy my sweets. I looked forward to what I thought was my independence, because, unlike most of the children in my peer group, I was the only one not to get "real pocket money" on Fridays like everybody else.

Practically everybody I knew worked, and did their chores in order to receive a pot of gold on that Friday teatime. At the time, I'd say the going rate was about a shilling in today's money about 12p, often topped up by a few pence with money gained from gambling. Gambling was something the children Devonport couldn't resist in fact, it caused more fights than I can remember, leading our headmaster to impose a total ban on a game known to us as pigeon toss. However, the game had absolutely nothing to do with and was completely devoid of any pigeon! Many years later somebody informed me that the games actual name was in fact, pitch-in-toss! Something that was obviously lost in translation because to us pigeon toss was the game that can make or break you, regarding your pocket money and prosperity. Getting back to why I was never one of the recipients of the Friday night pocket money pay out, was because my grandmother believed I was far too good to work! Reason being my Gran was from an older generation than most of my friends' parents. They were mostly only small children in the war, but she was an adult in the war and remembered the hardship and forever having to go without.

I know it's a terrible example to set for a child; however, I am what you would call a classic 100% solid gold "Boomer". The children who were born after the Second World War, not directly after because people were still suffering great hardship and restrictions like the rationing food, that carried on with the use of the treasured "ration book"? Years after the war had ended, the boomer child like me arrived when Britain had started to rebuild, when the food was plentiful and their people fully employed. Now living in decent clean accommodation, with the fledgling National Health Service running at full strength, employment was in abundance.

Our parents, who suffered all those years of great hardship, now had money and decided enough was enough; it was time to splash out.

Especially where their children were concerned. In other words, they spoilt us rotten! The term (Ruined) was the Plymouth nickname for a thoroughly indulged child.

A title, our parents wore like a badge of honour, because ruining your child was a sign of affluence and prosperity. The boomer children had everything handed down to them on a silver plate; reason being their parents or grandparents were absolutely fed up with years of scrimping and saving. Like my grandmother they had decided to live a little. It was more like live a lot! Considering the fact Gran was pissed every single day of my childhood, she was functioning, well enough to work and hold down a job keeping our house spotlessly clean

Most of all she took care of me, I'd say my Gran was constantly sedated with alcohol. Luckily enough for me, Gran was relatively peaceful and gushing in drink. Some of my friends didn't fare so well, some had parents who were real nasty in drink, or parents who would spend the weekly food money in one of Devonport's

Many pubs, leading to some being secretly neglected, I say secretly because any abuse noticed by the community would be dealt with immediately and harshly.

They policed themselves, there was absolutely no need for the welfare services to be involved, one whiff of neglect or cruelty you could expect your door literally kicked in off its hinges, and then get a good old-fashioned pasting from your friendly neighbours! I've seen this happen on many occasions. However, surprisingly, what I witnessed is after your door has been kicked in and your body had been "pasted the living daylights out of" by the local Women's mafia, you would more than often find yourself confined to your sofa, your house scrubbed from top to bottom. Your children washed and fed your food cupboard filled plus your windows and the said bashed down door fixed by the local handyman.

Then you'd get your one-off warning of "follow this example, you've learnt your lesson" now so carry on, and all would be forgotten. In all the years I lived there I never once witnessed anybody regress back into their old ways. The Devonport community really did police and look after itself. It was a symbiotic society. Everybody needed everybody else. The community believed that if everybody gave one item of food to a hard up person, or the person who was down on their luck due to a job loss would have more than enough to feed their family for a few weeks or more, and it worked. The same went for school uniforms, bedding, workman's tools, everything was provided for by our community.

The more I think about it, I've come to realise that Devonport was more like a communist micro community, and that was my life. I didn't really feel the need to move and go off into the world for a better life, because I had one and was exactly where I belonged in Devonport. I had a massive family, with hundreds of friends who I am still in contact with today, they've always been there and it looks like they always will be, I suppose this is what being raised in a tribe or a clan is like.

Outsiders were certainly not welcome by the people of Mount Wise. They were highly suspicious of strangers. To outsiders, they appeared guarded, moody and downright unfriendly; they often came over as very hostile. I've heard them described as "nasty bastards", on many occasions. Thinking back they may have been just been a tad bit on the greedy side protecting Mount wise from the outside world. They saw it as their land, regarding the fact that the area is one of the jewels of Plymouth geographically.

It truly was, or I should state is stunning. In my days especially, with beautiful clear clean water within touching distance, and overlooked by Mount Edgecombe, a Sprawling Cornish country estate once owned by histories hero and the saviours of England from the murderous tyrannical Spanish invaders, Our tiny little harbour, which looks small but is apparently the deepest sea water harbour in the world is guarded and looked over by an impressive massive statue of what Devonport folk refer to as our King Billy, who happens to be one of Britain's great kings, William of Orange, who took a liking to Plymouth.

But the arrival of a new kind of King, looked like he was going to destroy it all.

The people of Devonport had to rise up and fight once again for their survival.

Chapter Nine

The End of Nathan

I was the talk of the town. Everybody saw him for what he was nothing more than a mouthpiece, who used threats and intimidation to get his way. However, didn't have the metal to back it up when the time came. People were still afraid of the silent retributions, and like myself took to going to bed with a bucket of water underneath the letterbox, just in case the coward decided to send his henchman to burn us in our sleep. Apart from that his reign of terror was almost over

One year to the day of our stand-off, my Alamo, my Waterloo, the coward Nathan Pickett, was dead! Not by the hands or actions of any of my friends or neighbours, he had succumbed to a phenomenon known as Pippa's Gran. Pippa is a long deceased drinking partner of mine who suffered from depression and alcoholism. Very often she would succumb to depression, often amplifying day-to-day situations. I remember one day, her telling me a story after she'd visited and poured her heart out to her Gran concerning a very nasty neighbour of hers. Asking her Grans advice on what to do about the situation. Apparently, Pippa's Gran stared out the window for a few seconds, paused and took a deep breath. She said, "Put it this way Pip from what I've seen of life. If someone is that evil, there was no more evil you can do to them. However, if somebody is that evil, there's only one thing you can do and that's just wait, because eventually they'll do it to themselves".

In other words, the moral of the story is whatever you can do; it will never be as bad as what they can do to themselves,

I can't remember exactly what day it was when I heard the news that Nathan had stolen a disabled person's car, like the rotten swine he was. However, God must have been watching the swine, because his stolen car was written off in a massive motorway pileup caused by him, as he was high on drugs at the time. However, Nathan wasn't dead at the time, he was rescued by the emergency services, stabilised and taken to hospital. Apparently, the doctors worked tirelessly through the night and saved his life. However, he did not come through this unscathed. He was left almost paraplegic due to the impact, and severity of the crash. Devonport was peaceful whilst he was healing and convalescing after the accident. Then the dreaded news came he was on his way back. The people who rejoiced were genuinely worried again, until we saw him. I actually thought being confined to an electric wheelchair may have changed him, but I suppose a bad egg is always a bad egg and he was just as horrible. If not more so, it wasn't long before he was ramming peoples legs in shops and insulting people in the local pub. However, at this point, he was rather uncool, especially to his masses of adoring minions and one by one they slowly deserted him.

In the end, it was left to his poor sister, and may I add his only friend and ally at the time, to take care of him. Not one single person would give him the time of day. He received no sympathy and was well aware behind his back, and I mean literally within earshot, people started to take the piss out of him.

He became the butt of jokes and snide remarks, Nathan found himself in a very, very hostile environment and he knew it. People then started to humiliate him every opportunity they got. I truly believe if he came out of hospital and showed some humility and tried to make amends ,the people of Devonport would have bent over backwards to help him.

Because one thing we do know how to do, and that is how to forgive. We always believe in lessons learned, and that a person can change their ways. That life is not static, and doesn't always run the right course, but he didn't obviously.

I remember hearing people, laughing excitedly. Normally that means somebody's got their hands on a piece of juicy news or gossip, and if it's loud that means permission for anybody to ask what the joke was, that was our way. One horrible rainy day, Nathan committed suicide, rather than face life I suppose. As mentioned, he was almost paraplegic. He was left only with the use of one arm really, and used that to drive his electric wheelchair. With that good arm took his overhead support, sling, and wrapped it around his neck tight enough to strangle himself when he lay back down. He was found the next morning and my community were elated.

I would be a liar, If I said I felt the tiniest bit of sympathy for him, I don't, never did, and I never will. If he kicked me, I probably would have been able to forgive or at least feel some sympathy. However, he attacked my dog in my eyes that's unforgivable in the next ten months many members of his gang died of accidental drug overdoses. Three, I know personally or I should say I knew their mothers, who I have great sympathy for, and did my best at the time to support each and every one of them. I suppose, in the case of Nathan Pickett it's best not to try and analyse the person or what makes them tick, just strip it all down to the basics with the understanding that some people are just born bad.. Nathan certainly was.

On the night of the would be King of Devonport's death. I remember the recounting the drama bit by bit, in graphic detail every single bit of the story to my brother over the phone. This was one of many of our conversations we had about my life in Devonport. My brother Joe wasn't only a good talker he was also an excellent listener as well. The one thing he never did was to overreact, especially when talking about bad boys or the would be gangsters of my world. Normally people's eyes would widen in surprise when told the story about my brush with the underworld, but not my Joe, it was like water off a ducks back, as far as he was concerned.

That I had almost single headedly taken on and defeated Devonport's equivalent of a would Capone and his gang, had little to no effect as far as Joe was concerned. To Joe I had been involved in nothing more than a play adult playground scrap. However, Joe was fun to talk to. I used to refer to him as the sister I never had. I could literally talk to him about anything, unlike most men he would have an opinion or interest on anything, especially anything that would be classed as women's talk, funny because it's a subject most men seem to avoid like the plague.

I can remember thinking, come on show a little bit of enthusiasm, after all I had been in a battle with a underworld criminal cartel! However, Joe seemed far more interested in the fact of how I'd managed to burn my head with a with my new hair straighteners! No matter what conversation or subject we were discussing, we always ended up talking about Joes favourite subject and that being women.

He absolutely loved women not just your classic beauties with big boobs, I'm talking about "all women" , old women, young women, black women, Latin women, Asian women, tall, women, skinny women, clever women, thick women,, even men dressed up as women, and his personal favourite downright nasty dirty women!

Joe could talk endlessly about women, and he could charm the pants off a nun. He studied and understood women, making them literally putty in his hands. Unfortunately, me included. To guide me off a conversation that he was not interested in, he would simply ask if I needed anything nice on our next shopping trip. Knowing that was like a red rag to a bull, asking me if I needed anything, because I always needed everything, even if I had an item with tags on in my wardrobe, I'd often find myself pursuing the same item, just to make sure I didn't run out, I have to have at least two of everything, I suppose I've got an underlying hoarder problem.

To this day, I still find it impossible to just buy one thing. My brother always ended our conversations with, I'll pop the money into your bank account, and that's how it was for me. Never having to worry about money, because one word from me, and my Joe would oblige. I never felt bad taking money off Joe, because after all, with him being a successful antiques dealer in London, it meant he had a fair bit of cash to throw about. In fact, he was so extravagant. If he saw something, even if it was of no use to him whatsoever, he would just buy it he spent ridiculous amounts of money on absolute crap!

A few days later after our none eventful conversation, the phone rang again with a very excited Joe on the end of the line. Blurting out. I've done it! My obvious reply was, done what you prat, as I chuckled down the phone. Booked you a holiday came the reply. Apparently, somewhere in our drunken conversations, I had mentioned that I would like to go to the Greek island of Zante? I was thinking I must've been really drunk at the time because I had absolutely no recollection of ever saying that I wanted to travel to Greece? However, a free holiday is a free holiday, seeing it already booked and paid for who was I to refuse. I slept on it that night I remember waking up really excited. I spent the day telling everyone about my all-expense paid holiday on the beautiful island of Zante. Yet another one of the expensive treats provided by my extravagant and impulsive half sibling.

And just like that, Joe disappeared! And when I say disappeared, I mean gone, literally vanished off the face of the earth.

Chapter Ten

The Visit

It took me in total four long painful heart wrenching years to find my Brother. Four years of phone calls and waiting for letters and four years of interrogating our mother! She had her story and she was sticking to it. Nothing I could say or do, could get the truth out of her lying mouth, because her story regarding my brother's absence, which was designed to protect me at the time I suppose, was an obvious stinking rotten lie and there was nothing at the time I could do about it. This all took place way before the Internet, so you can understand how hard and frustrating it was for me. Those four bloody years I spent looking for my Brother Joe almost killed me it was literally eating me away until.

When I eventually found him, he was languishing at her Majesty's pleasure in the Verne maximum security prison! His sentence was life my funny, generous, handsome Brother looked like he was going to be incarcerated for eternity. However, going on to study the legal system, I found out that a "life sentence" is mostly given to murders. It means you've taken a life not that you will be incarcerated for life and is to this day.

It the only sentence that a judge can hand down to somebody who's killed, with Actus-Reus and Men's-Rea, in Layman's terms committed the crime with a guilty act and a guilty mind. In fact, many premeditated murderers have spent less time in prison than thieves! As in the case of the great train robbery, who spent I believe over 40 years in prison for their crimes, leading many of us to believe that crimes against property and finance are dealt with far more severely than crimes against the actual person. Fortunately, Joe was sentenced to the same amount of years in prison, about 14 years if I remember rightly? However, it was not classed as a life sentence due to the fact he had not killed anybody. Thank God!

My delightful charismatic brother, the person who could charm the pants off a nun was in fact a bank robber. No, let's give him his full total, Joe was, in fact, an armed bank robber. I found out he'd been knocking off banks and post offices for donkey's years. Starting his criminal career at 16 years old. Meeting my Joe in prison was like meeting a completely different person. Gone was his beautiful conditioned hair, his complexion was grey, his eyes were lifeless, and his clothes were practically rags. What affected me most, was the fact his spark, that excitable spark that made up Joe. Had vanished completely. He sat across from me biting his once perfectly manicured nails, barely able to make eye contact with me.

Truthfully, I didn't know what to say, or even how to say it, I could feel a beautiful thing was over and that we were finished. I received a letter from mother a week later, stating that Joe wanted me to get on with my life, and forget him. He asked me not to write or request a visit. I remember; thinking to myself, get on with my life, what life? Over the next few months, I started to evaluate the shit out of my life, or the obvious lack of it now that Joe was gone.

Chapter Eleven

Ass Kicking Time

The people of Devonport were tough, not I'll rough you up tough. Real tough if that makes any sense. We were brought up with the philosophy of "Ask don't get, don't ask don't want". To an outsider, Devonport people were very hard to understand. A confusing clan of people, who very often appeared to talk in riddles. If I was to ever give any advice to an outsider, it would be to reverse everything they say or do, be well prepared for anything and everything. Our motivation came in the form of a swift kick up the ass! We were given absolutely no form of sympathy, and if there was even a tiny hint of feeling sorry for yourself it could make you an outcast in seconds.

It was a community decision on who was to receive sympathy. After all sympathy was in short supply in Devonport. In their eyes they had to distribute it sparingly, it was rationed. It was the community, who decided who was to be on the receiving end of any sympathy, which was to be awarded the sympathy, and exactly how much sympathy you were entitled to was awarded by your street. Unfortunately for those of us, who detest empathy, "you're up shit creek without a paddle". Because once the community have made their decision, and you have been ordered that "swift kick up the arse" meaning the community had bent over backwards to help you, choice was out of your hands.

The crying actual water out of one's eyes was strictly forbidden, unless it was the result of laughing too much crying

71

with laughter. This was classed as one of Devonport's favourite pastimes. "I pissed myself, laughing!" Tears of happiness were also permitted. This action had to be tastefully completed with a dignified dab under each eye. I was going to say with a tissue or a hanky, but in truth, it was mainly your sleeve.

Last but not least, the rage cry, or the temper cry could be, and is expected at times of severe distress. In the past I have personally witnessed this frightening tantrum especially when the long waited for giro check has failed to turn up. This sort of enraged intense crying can also affect the use of your limbs, with arms grabbing, punching and throwing anything in sight along with pulling your own hair out in chunks! This can affect both men and women, OAP's even the kids, damn I've even seen their animals do it. Having achieved all that, you can then refer to the good old Devonport saying, "I went soddin ballistic!" Every other form of crying was expected to be done in private. Jokes aside this was the Devonport way!

"Did you ever see a wild thing, feeling sorry for its self?

A poem bye (D. H. Lawrence). I believe, should be on the people of Devonport's unofficial coat of arms.

Chapter Twelve

Ballistic Missile

I would hope by now the reader would have a fair understanding of my background, my close-knit environment, my upbringing and the people I consider to have been my extended family. The important thing was we stuck together through thick and thin, so what I did next in shock value was actually like dropping a virtual ballistic missile in the middle of Devonport. I remember one day walking home clutching a packet of fags, I'd just purchased from a local corner shop, that was only a five minute walk away. However, in Devonport that five minute could easily turn into half an hour. On occasions, I've been known to take up to 2 to 3 hours on that short five minute trip, very often the temptation of the gossip proved too much and was too far too tasty to ignore resulting in lengthy conversations sat down on what we called "the wall ". There were actually there were lot of walls in Pembroke Street, the very street I was born. Pembroke Street was designed after the war, a flag ship of modern development to provide the people of with safe clean homes.

Two patches of grass that lay between two blocks of flats, sort of like a massive concrete bench where people sat and watched over their children playing. I wouldn't like to count the amount of hours I sat to gossip, laughed with friends, got drunk, and even consumed my Sunday roast dinner on that wall. Me being preoccupied that day the wall was of no consequence, and I easily resisted the temptation to "poke my ass down", The Devonport invitation to sit down, so I could gossip. No, that day I was completely preoccupied.

Nothing was making sense. I've posted previously that I'm naturally gifted in judging the situation, reading the room, and most of all reading people. I've got a sixth sense when it comes to things like that, but not today because just like that, I had decided to go back to school. Why, I do not know? I bloody hated the bloody place, especially after I found myself expelled. I'd like to say it was for a monumental hilarious prank, that would go down in the school's history, but now I am old enough to admit I thoroughly deserved my punishment. However, to this day, I wish I'd been a bit slyer in taking my revenge on the teacher I clouted around the ear. I could follow up that slap with a good old-fashioned boot up the crack of her ass, because she was truly a monster, an evil sadistic jealous bitch. I'd like to say, I've mellowed concerning my juvenile hatred of her but I've not, not one bit and blame her solely for my terrible start on the careers ladder. Not only did I come from a comprehensive education, which was basically the creation of the factory workforce. But because of my expulsion, I didn't even get a leavers letter which was normally handed to your first employer. However, in those days and me being excellent in exaggeration and charm, I managed to gain meaningful employment due to the fact, I spent my last year at school in a place called a RASLA unit an abbreviation from, raising of school leaving age, which came as a total shock to us all who were expected to leave school and start work at the age of 15.

The government increased the age to 16 literally overnight, I know many people who were due to start work and had to withdraw their application for a job, only to spend another pointless and I mean pointless twelve months doing nothing, because we were not taking any examinations at school. I was particularly shocked considering the fact I managed to get myself expelled. From what I thought was only going to be another two weeks before I was due to leave school anyway, only to find I had another 12 months to complete. It was a total mess.

Fed up with working, I did what most young girls even to this day in some cases did, and that was to get myself pregnant. The government would support you practically forever. That was then not now thankfully. In the next 10 years I produce four babies. However, after producing these four beautiful bundles of joy, I realised I did not like babies! In fact, I just couldn't see the point of them. They just lay there, looking cute and demanding food; However, I made sure everything was perfect food, clothes, outings. Truthfully, I had no other choice, unless I wanted to be ceremoniously, beaten within an inch of my life and ostracised by my community.

In truth, I could not abandon anything helpless whether I liked it or not. However, all was not lost when I realised, I only disliked babies because of the lack of interaction. I actually really liked them when they grew into little kids. Not having a maternal bone in my body, the children were able to explore more than most, I saw them as little people not helpless, tiny versions of their parents. Their upbringing made them gutsy, willing to have a go at almost anything. I have noticed, they've all developed my instinct to defend weaker people and each and every one of them have inherited my true love of the animal kingdom.

All the complaints I've had from them over the years make me chuckle because they are more like me than they could ever imagine. All are too clever for their old good sometimes. Gran could never decide if I was clever or crafty? However, in the end decided I was a bit of both and that I would probably be okay in life, especially being able to judge situations and read the room. They all have impeccable manners and I'm proud to say from a very early age I could take them anywhere. However, like me, they can turn on a pin if crossed.

What my grandmother never considered in a million years, or anybody else for that matter, including myself, was the fact I could be academically clever. Now that was a whole different ballgame, so for my next trick at the age of almost 30, I decided to find out and rocked my whole community by returning to school. In fact, I became the talk of the town, leaving everybody completely gobsmacked! Everybody was talking about, "Lizzie is going back to school ", and for the first time I was the butt of everybody's jokes. In fact, I'd made myself, a bloody laughing stock. Me of all people! I was highly respected, and one of the backbones of my clan. In fact, it wasn't technically school, it was a college where I sat and took my first formal exam, GCSE Law.

Hells Bells, I did something nobody in my environment had done, as academic qualifications were strictly only for grammar school pupils, those who passed their 11+. Remember we were the secondary modern factory fodder. The workers, the ones who got their hands dirty. The ones on the foot, were the officers were on horseback. We were ones who served the tables, rather than be served. We were the ones who dressed, fed and cared for others. All decided by one, one hour exam at the age of 11. That was your lot, for the rest of your life. One hour, one stinking rotten hour. I once read that a revolution can start with just one act of defiance. Well, I had defied every one of those teachers who called me thick, just because I was born on a run-down council estate!

Years later, when I was sat in one of my many political history lectures, I was told to really understand the meaning of the word revolution, was to just see it as just meaning to change, and I suppose that's what was happening, and what happened to me. I was changing, not changing me as a person, just my thought process of the big world outside of Devonport. Me being me, I thought you've taken the first step and got yourself a GCSE and passed with a good mark (B plus), why don't you just see what's around the corner?

And that's exactly what I did. I went from college GCSEs onto higher education and started my A-levels. Passed all with flying colours, ending up in university not once, but twice, after having total fallout with my law degree. I was far too Devonport to be taking any crap mitigations on how, and why a defendant behaved a certain way. Criminal defence lawyer was the pigeon hole I was placed in, probably because my years growing up on a council estate had given me the ability to argue till the cows came home, never to back down, and how to talk the ass end of a donkey!

All those years of me lying and deceiving, council, officials, the rent man, debt collectors, and the police, had perfectly positioned me for a job in the law. Believe it or not one of the tests you take to see what position you best be suited to in law is the army's SAS survival course, I was a perfect killing machine and I could get the job done.

Chapter Thirteen

College Days

Without a doubt, being brought up on a council estate, there's one thing you do know what to do really well, and that's how to survive. But as far as I was concerned, the law I was studying was an ass. Unfortunately, looking at a lot of the terrible situations from my point of view, because of my upbringing, I would say 50% of the victims could have saved themselves an awful lot of trouble if they just applied council estate logic, and that is to trust no one but your close friends and family.

More than often victims of fraud are well brought up people from good families, who have never struggled or suffered a tiny bit of hardship in their lives. They don't understand the survival instinct of others. Very often I found myself in court absolutely seething with temper, not at the perpetrator, but at the victim. In Devonport, we would say how you could you have been so bloody stupid! However, naiveté often comes before stupidity, as far as I'm concerned,

 Most definitely the straw that broke the camel's back for me, was a case of a lovely young family, a modern progressive family out of the kindness of their own hearts took a homeless man into their house, probably all the time bragging to their friends of the self-righteousness of helping others who are down on their luck. To cut a long story short because the last thing I want to do is dramatize the situation, is the fact the stupid bloody idiots, not only took an unknown homeless man into their family home, they also provided him with a bed in their baby sons bedroom!

I really don't need to dwell on what happened next, apart from the fact; because of their stupidity they no longer have a son. Being what I class as a "normal person", with average common sense, I found myself having no sympathy for them. Regardless; it was the end of the legal profession for me as far as I was concerned, there were no mitigating circumstances for either the victim or the perpetrator. I was too opinionated by my upbringing up to be trusting and unbiased. I remember being asked by my tutor, my thoughts on how I would defend that child murderer, a question that he had stated would probably be hard for me to answer? Hard? Not sodding hard, I thought not hard this one is easy mate; I'd bloody strangle the twat! This was not the answer my college middle-class educator was expecting I could tell by the shocked look in his eyes.

This is probably why they keep the lower working classes out of the legal profession. Reason being honesty, we are too bloody honest, black and white, right and wrong. I'm afraid there is no in between on a council estate. So, I left. Over the next few years, I drifted between jobs and also to my surprise managed to stick to a calorie controlled diet. I have quite an obsessive nature, so when I put my mind to something I normally overly succeed and managed to drop a whopping six stone being quite tall with large shoulders, and obviously my heavy African bones. I found myself. Around the size 10/12 dress mark, my baby face and puppy fat had disappeared. Looking back at the photographs without boasting, I was a bit of a babe as they say. That made me even more lethal to men, which is just as well because my second husband was just about to get the boot.

Tom Berk was an ex-royal Marine, Falklands war veteran. Blonde, Viking looking like most men of Cornish stock. Who, after the war joined one of many of the cable laying gangs who were being paid a vast amount of money to prepare Britain for the coming Internet revolution, which meant he travelled an awful lot. The pay equalled the inconvenience of being away from home for great lengths of time. It was a great life and very attractive to an ex-serviceman. Being in a large group of comrades, all doing the same job. However, there's an old saying when the "cats away the mice will play" Play they did, all of them. If they were in the Royal Navy in Plymouth, we would say that they had "a girl in every port." Also, a brigade of unsuspecting wives sat happily at home looking after the children. However, I was just waiting for my old man to trip up, and trip up he did. Now any normal woman and I've seen it hundreds of times, would be devastated. Crying themselves to sleep every night, or barring the rogue from the house, and then giving in after being promised it will never happen again. Or having a practical nervous breakdown, not eating and losing weight plus losing all self-respect in the process, that often follows this form of grieving.

And then we have me, who was by nature, was a predator. I found out Tom had been dipping his wick on a Sunday morning in the seaside town of Blackpool. Whilst on one of my weekend visits instead of crying, wailing and acting, like any other, "normal woman" would, I found myself being overly attentive to my dear husband Tom, something he was not used to at all. He must have bitterly regretted what he had done because I don't remember him looking at me with softness in his eyes like he did that day. He was probably thinking at the time why the hell have I shagged someone else, my Lizzie is perfect. But I was far from bloody perfect, because all day, and I mean all bloody day, I kept up the facade and gave him the biggest loving farewell kiss a wife could plant on her departing husband. All the time unbeknown to Tom, it was to be the last time he would ever be kissed by me. Let's call it the kiss of death, like the black spot as far as I was concerned, that man was marked! The asshole!

Revenge is sweet, and revenge is a dish best served cold, not in the heat of the moment. It has far more impact. So over the next 24 hours with the help of my friend Gig Jones, I systematically emptied every single penny from Toms bank account. I can remember to this day, the bank clerk saying are you sure you want the last 32p, when making my last transaction. Yes please, I want all of it, was my answer. By this time, although not from Devonport, Gig, executed the piss myself, laughing stance, of grabbing your crutch to hold in her pee. She had the, pissing yourself laughing, position to perfection. Even she couldn't believe the lengths I was prepared to go, and trust me I was prepared to go to get right up to the line in order to get the very last penny out of that man, in order to seal my revenge.

The morning Tom realised I'd cleaned out his bank account, he was said to be distraught. But not just your normal distraught, apparently, he was bloody frantic. Because of all the days to run out of money, today was going to be his worst. That day, of all days, dear old Tom not only had to settle his hotel bill, book another hotel and fill up his car with enough petrol for the 400 mile trip to Scotland in order to begin his next job.

When he caught up with me, and he finally did, his screams were, "it was like you bloody planned it" all the time! I took this as a compliment, but not really, it was just a lucky coincidence. He also accused me of being as" hard as nails" to be able to spend 24 loved up hours with him, while all the time knowing exactly what he had done! Just to throw him off the track, or give him any warning that I had found out about his goings on.

In truth I loved every minute of it, the bitch inside me was working overdrive. When the stories got back of that morning and how that poor little innocent Tom had actually cried real tears of frustration and devastation outside of his bank, if I remember correctly, he was heard saying, "lizzies stitched me up like a sodden kipper!" The man who witnessed this was Gig Jones's own husband, Simple Steven. Who took great delight in forwarding the information back to us, saying that no-one who saw this broken man's tantrum could keep a straight face! Lol … And that was the end of Tom everyone deserves a second chance apart from a cheat and a liar! Granny Blanche taught me that.

Chapter Fourteen

Roxanne

After Tom, I decided I have nothing else better to do and decided to go back to college and try something different. But this time, I was playing with the idea of teaching the arts; poetry, history and political history were to be my next adventure. Up to that point, I didn't see myself as a deep thinker, or the sort of person who could sit for hours looking up into the sky, asking the question why, or trying to analyse the woes of the world. After all I was, and still am a very matter-of-fact, black is black and white is white kind of person. However, if I was going to teach, I realised I was probably going to have to have a lot more empathy.

The college were happy to accept me, especially seeing they needed to get their quota filled up with mature students for that year. The first day I arrived at the beginning of term, everything was completely different from the first time I enrolled. After being through the whole process of enrolment, this time I was totally relaxed. Carrying just one notepad and pen. Nothing like the first time where I arrived, with a large briefcase filled to the brim with the contents of Smith's stationary store. No, it was the first day; all I needed was a pen to jot down any notes that would be of importance to me in the coming days. Yes, I was a veteran and an old hat at this malarkey.

The class started filling up, one by one with all kinds of people. Me being a people watcher enjoyed analysing each one as they entered. Some nervous, obviously because after all

83

starting a new school for anyone can be daunting, especially daunting for those who have been out of the educational system for years. Then there were the couple who look down their nose at everybody with the attitude of I'm really too good for all this shit, just give me my degree now! Then I looked up and there she was entering the room like the queen, Roxanne (Roxy) I don't know if I should have laughed or ran, knowing what I know now, because in had walked my kindred spirit or should I say my partner in crime? From the outside, we had absolutely nothing in common. From the outside we looked like we were from different solar systems never mind the planets. To look at Roxanne was willowy tall, almost 6 feet, where I was 5 foot six, she was slim where I was chubby, she had long, blonde hair, where I had a tamed Afro, she had piercing pale blue eyes that looked right through you, I had large, dark seductive, come to bed eyes.

Roxanne was privately educated, I was a secondary modern woman, she grew up in a country picture book cottage, I was from the dreaded concrete, council estate. She was as posh as the Queen, where I proudly held on to my West Country accent. To top it, all I had extremely good manners and empathy for others. Where Roxanne was dismissive and very often came over as damn right rude and very cold. Hopefully you will have got the picture by now. But as the old saying goes, opposites attract!

I don't often succumb to fantasising, but I found myself very often, wondering and pondering the fact that me and Roxanne were probably connected in a former life. Whatever it was, or should I say is, there is definitely an invisible connection between us both. Practically 90% I would even go farther, and say 95% of people who have ever met Roxanne hated her guts and all the time I've known her I've never heard anybody even once say a good thing about her.

 And the best bit about Roxanne was, she didn't care. She's probably the only person I've ever met, who really didn't care what others thought of her. After the initial niceties of our very first meeting, it didn't take long for me and this vixen to get down to business.

After the niceties were out of the way, we hit the ground running. Later I understood completely why I was so attracted to Roxanne; it was the fact we're practically identical in one area of our personalities. We were both hedonists, both selfish pleasure seekers, who had had to spend years in training, hiding our guilty secret from our friends and family. We both had found someone who completely understood that need to be completely selfish. I later found out through observation something she didn't really try to hide from me, and that was Roxanne was a rampant nymphomaniac.

When I say rampant to put it bluntly, I mean the girl was absolutely gagging for it, morning noon and night! No joke, she wasn't even bothered what the guys look like, how much money they had, if they were married or not. Worst of all she didn't even care if she fancied them or not, or the other way around. Roxanne called men human vibrators, and used them a lot more than they used her. Remembering the amount of broken heart she left in her wake, she was a total pariah. She even managed to make my eyes water on a few occasions, and I truthfully always thought of myself as being shockable, However, this girl had written the book on bad behaviour, when it came down to morals.

She was in fact married to a guy in the Navy. Not that that stopped her. In fact, I often wondered if he was in on it in some way. Nowadays, I would be convinced that there was a motion detector camera hidden above one of her wardrobes, allowing him to get his kicks thousands of miles away. Anyway, I didn't care I was having the time of my life. I forgot to mention Roxanne was not only tall and attractive; she was rich as well and thought nothing of splashing her cash about, especially on vodka, taxis and nightclubs! We were practically eating our conquest up, Roxanne sexually, me emotionally, but we were both on a massive power trip.

However, after five days of hard clubbing, I realised I needed a rest. I wanted to put my feet up, dressed in my old scruffy jogging bottoms and spend the evening stuffing my face with crap whilst watching shitty TV programmes, but oh no, Roxanne was having none of it. In fact, I remember cringing when the phone rang because I knew exactly what was about to happen, and why. Roxanne wanted to go out, not for the drink because she practically had a brewery in her house, but I knew that old uncontrollable urge had hit her, Roxanne was horny, as simple as that.

She literally barked down the phone you'll enjoy yourself when you get a drink in side of you. Mine was a tea total house, I never once up to that point drank alcohol in the house, and I never ever drank alcohol alone.

To me, downing copious amounts of alcohol, went hand-in-hand with the party scene, apart from that I had no other use for alcoholic drinks. Probably the fear of ending up like my train wreck of an alcoholic mentally ill mother, who by that time was a total recluse, suffering with agoraphobia as long as she had her alcohol, she didn't care.

It was always terribly hard to say no to Roxanne, so in good old Devonport terms, I got my "glad rags" on and waited for the taxi. She always provided…

Chapter Fifteen

Cardiff Born

I often wonder where I would be right now if I had resisted Roxanne's offer. I often thank Roxanne from the bottom of my heart for making that offer. Because that was the night over thirty years ago when my life changed completely, spinning me in a completely different direction to the one I had been going. It's taken me to places I'd never been before, forcing me to re-evaluate everything.

Because absolutely nobody knows what's around the corner, or what we could lose if we don't take that invisible corner, without that turn good or bad you will never find out. It's those sliding doors moments that can give us that once in a lifetime chance. A coincidence brought about by millions of variations, mistakes, and dreams.

By 11:30 that night, I was safely and stubbornly installed on my favourite bar stool. My perch was perfectly positioned for me to entertain myself in the coming hours, doing what I'd like to do best, and that was people watching.

I could also view the door, the dance floor and the toilets, plus having the easy access to the bar. Sort of like the lookout post in the old Wild West movies. At this time, Roxanne was fluttering like the social butterfly she was, for a better description would be more like a predatory animal, looking to pick off the weaker prey at the back of the pack. Through my years of good adult potty training mixed with my utter dislike of public conveniences, once I put my ass down on my perch I never moved, however, this night of all nights I was absolutely dying for a pee, and that meant one thing I was going lose my vantage point.

I think I spent about half an hour trying to resist going to that ladies loo. Eventually, I'd given in to the uncontrollable urge plus the fear that one cough would result in me pissing myself leaking. I reluctantly gave up my territory, abandoning my stool. Inside the ladies toilet the usual shenanigans we're taking place. Normally there was at least one girl crying her eyes out over a man, someone who drank too much being sick all over the cubical floor, older girls trying to break up a cat fight, plus the ceremonial queue for the few mirrors we have in the ladies toilets.

In those days, hardly any one closed the cubicle doors, it was a place where you could hold court, all the time chatting and debating with your friends whilst taking a pee. I hated it then, and I hate it now the thought of sitting on a toilet seat that a stranger had been sitting pants down on to do their business. Over the years, I have perfected the art of straddling up to go, not like a man would taking a pee. I could pee standing up all the time holding my knickers out of the way of my golden shower, because of my unorthodox preferred method of urination, my toilet door was always firmly locked for obvious reasons. If I didn't mind sitting on a dirty toilet seat, I probably would have spent a little more time in there that night because I was in no rush to get back out knowing full well my precious lookout point would be gone.

By this point, I was thoroughly pissed off. Not only did I not want to go out that night, I'd also lost my preferred location and the thought of standing on the edge of the dancefloor watching Roxanne getting groped did not appeal to me at all.

89

After all, I was supposed to be sat in my scruffy, jogging, bottoms that night pigging out on chocolates and watching second rate soap operas, thinking to myself all this was Roxanne's fault. By now my blood was boiling, I was simply not in the mood. To make matters worse, I needed a drink, not that I actually needed a drink. I needed something in my hands so I didn't look like a complete and utter saddo or even worse a skint wallflower.

I was in a foul mood as I made my way to the bar. I can remember telling at least four men who had tried their luck and propositioned me to piss off. Jesus Christ, the bar was four or five people deep when I finally got there. Once there I realised it was probably going to take me another bloody half an hour just to get a soddin drink! So, I gave up, called-time, and stood there like a complete and utter grumpy gut. Enough was enough! It was then it happened.

My night had gone well and truly tits up! Another old Devonport saying for "disaster". Roxanne as usual, was right in the middle of a feeding frenzy of would be drunk suitors, and would have probably wouldn't even noticed if I had gone. She was dressed in a skin tight, black mini dress, which barely covered her ass and leather over the knee black boots. Her blonde hair extensions were so long they practically reached to the level of her hemline. She actually didn't need any make up, because her face was the last thing men were looking at. My Granny Blanche had a saying concerning facial beauty, "you don't look at the mantel piece when you're poking the fire". Unbeknown to these would be bed mates, the winner or winners, were about to receive 3rd° degree burns from a fire that would probably take them years to recover from.

I can remember, grinning, thinking bloody stupid men, it serves them right. No, my mind was made up. I was going home I was even more pissed off at the thought of paying for my own taxi, that pissed me off even more. Jesus, I was in a foul mood. Then I saw him just sitting there, a guy looking like he didn't have a care in the bloody world, and sitting very comfortable on my bloody bar stool as well! The cheeky sod.

Anybody who remembers the disco scene of the 80s and 90s will know it's an environment, combining high energy and fun. The people's mood, governed by the experienced DJ's of the day, who kept your blood pumping until the last half an hour. It was that last 30 minutes you would see practically every man on his feet, because that's when the slow dances come on, and they could legitimately get their hands on a woman for free, the dreaded slow dance. Something I refused point blankly to participate in, after almost 15 years on the disco scene unlike most girls, I was not in any shape or form interested, or flattered at the thought of a bloke showing me attention just before kicking out time.

These women were too stupid to realise when a man shows you attention fifteen minutes before closing time, he's actually managed to save himself a fortune buying you drinks. But not me, you would have to get up early to catch Lizzie out with a trick like that.

Us real Devonport girls were crafty; I'd seen it all before meaning, (no drink, no chance!) Not only was this guy sat on my favourite bar stool, the cheeky bastard was wiggling his finger beckoning me over, I was absolutely flaming, no one and I mean no one, puts me at their beck and call... I was going to give this one a piece of my mind before I left... in those days to look cool, and to keep up the facade of confidence you moved slowly, but I found myself almost jumping to attention at his request. Thinking back, I had done no evaluation of his looks, something quite out of character for me, after all that was unimportant seeing I'd only moved in order to give him a peace of mind for stealing my beloved bar stool. I was weaponised, locked and loaded, primed, oh boy was he going to get it with both barrels? Devonport terminology, to "prepare yourself for hell" I don't normally like getting too close to men I don't know, physically plus being brought up on a council estate, you learn not to invade other people's personal space. However, on this occasion I found myself almost nose to nose with this bar stool thief. All I could think of he was very brave, drunk or very stupid, because he didn't flinch a bit! I have always prided myself on looking formidable. What came next is etched on my brain, because with the biggest smile, he held up his glass and said can I buy you a drink? Even my reply of, do I look bloody skint? Didn't seem to flummox him one bit.

To which he just laughed in amusement, which through me even more. The horror that I may have to back down from a confrontation or lose an argument before I'd even started was dawning on me. After all, I was a control freak and used to everything going my way. Put it this way, it was either my way, or the highway! I don't know if it was fate, an unknown entity or God's intervention, but the unthinkable happened because right behind me, inches from my buttocks, a bar stool became vacant, it must've been instinct I suppose? Because I plonked my ass firmly down. Surprised because it's the very last thing I would do, and that would be to sit down with my enemy.

I was thinking Jesus Christ, I was only here to give him a piece of my mind before I left, now I find myself sitting in close proximity to you, like a couple. I was in an unknown battle with an unknown opponent; I could sense I was losing it as well, so I did nothing. I'd previously watched a David Attenborough program, where he featured an animal who pretended to be dead in order to escape its prey, it must of unconsciously stuck in my mind I kept my mouth shut. Within ten minutes I practically knew his life story, I knew his ins and outs, his likes and dislikes, I was astounded how he unashamedly revealed the that he liked black girls and found them far more attractive than any other race. Boy could this bloke talk…

My Gran, Who denied ever using swear words, would have summed him up in one sentence of, "having more mouth than a cows, got tits. I found myself mesmerised by his beautiful soft Welsh accent. I didn't realise at the time that I was smiling, and interacting with his stories, that I was being led by his conversation, instead of me controlling everything like I normally did. It was a long time after, that did I realise that I had let him do something that I am normally 100% on my Guard with and that's physical boundaries. I didn't realise I was allowing him to touch me whilst in conversation, not in a sexual way, but the way, close friends, family or people who have a deep love and affection for each other would touch, shoulders, arms, hands hair, cheeks. And just like that I had fallen completely and utterly in love!

He hadn't just invaded my space. He, this young Welshman had completely moved into my life.

Chapter Sixteen

Welsh and Gran

Fifteen months later, we were married. Twenty three months later, I gave birth to his daughter. Meeting my Welshman (Welsh) was like opening a window to a room that has been closed and neglected for years. With the power of a hurricane blowing, and tearing all the old junk away followed by a cleansing rain, washing and sterilising the past grime that had built up over the past.

Me and Welsh from the first day we met became almost like conjoined twins, barely leaving one another's side; however, this was no mills and boon romance this was full throttle, pure, adrenaline, fun! At the beginning of our relationship, I still owned a flat that I have been renting out and being a sensible Devonport girl, wary of introducing a strange man to the children, I decided not to look for a new tenant. If I was dramatic, I would have called it our love nest, but it was far more than that. It literally became our playground, gone were the pubs and nightclubs, gone discotheques and the hustle and bustle of Plymouth's Notorious union Street, we literally wrote the book on staying in is the new going out.

We'd shop for hours in Marks & Spencer's, for the food we were going to eat that night. Welsh is a big lad and absolutely loved his food. My teetotal at home life soon went out the window, resulting in me and Welsh drunkenly dancing till dawn on many occasions. We hardly ever watched TV or movies; we just filled our lives with music and laughter. We told jokes. Gossiping for hours, we talked about everything and anything that took our fancy. We were quickly becoming a pair, a double act, each fulfilling each other's needs. He was, and still is the best friend I've ever had.

Do I believe in love at first sight? To be perfectly honest with you, I'm not sure I fully understand instant attraction. I fully understand physically fancying the pants off someone, I understand infatuation. But, as I mentioned earlier, if you have to bang on about your romantic stories, you're probably not living in a true love story if that makes any sense? Years passed, Welsh said goodbye to the Navy and we decided we both needed something different. A move was out of the question because my dear Old Granny Blanche had become increasingly old and frail. I spent hours trying to convince her to move in with us, but she soon cottoned on to the fact I wanted to leave Devonport for pastures new. I don't know if she had forgotten, or just didn't care anymore about bad language, but she promptly told me to stick my offer right up my effin arse. I took that as a definite No!

I was tied down by her, and there was nothing I could do about it. The old witch had me over a barrel. A few weeks later, she rang me up all excited giggling that she was a young woman again, due to the fact her periods had returned! My head was spinning because I knew at her age this could mean only one thing. Getting her to see a doctor proved to be a monumental task due to the fact, she absolutely hated them.

She once told me that after fifty, if they take you into hospital, that's it, you'll never come out again, like the film Logan's Run with everybody over a certain age, were deemed a burden to their society, so once their youth was gone, they were disposed of. We finally got the diagnosis of cervical cancer, this affected Gran greatly, believing the Old wives tales that cervical cancer was only contracted only by loose women, prostitutes and slags as she called them. Thankfully it didn't take long. In truth, I believe she made her decision; time was up and just stopped breathing.

To this day, I remember a very strange incident concerning the build up to grans departure. Before we go any further, I want to state categorically, I do not believe in the supernatural.

I did when I was younger, however that was probably the result of watching too many hammer horror movies. As I grew up, and got older, I became more scientific, questioning, analysing and getting to the bottom of what are basically nothing more, but adult fairy tales. Gran was rapidly coming to the end, although at that time, I didn't know it. Obviously, it was sitting at the back of my mind along with the rest of the crap I was not prepared to address at the time.

Like it or not, her life clock was ticking, and our time together on this planet was coming to an end, physically that is. I truly believe by telling the story of all those who have passed makes them all very much alive to me today. I remember entering Grannies house through the back door, which she never kept locked. I could see her asleep in her chair as normal, me being fully used to the hustle and bustle of Devonport, I never actually ever noticed that it was quite noisy in her little flat throughout the day, well not until I stepped over her doorstep that day and everything fell silent. Not your quiet silence, but a kind of nothing silent, if that makes any sense? As I explained earlier, I am a pragmatic person and life is either black or white, there is right and wrong, or hot or cold.

But I'll never forget entering her room that day, because Granny Blanche had an aura of light around her like a thick luminescent mist or fog. There was an overwhelming presence, of what I cannot fathom. However, my feelings at the time were of one that I was interrupting something special and that I was definitely not meant to be there. An unconscious voice kept telling me that I was disturbing an important process. That I had gate crashed something beautiful and full of peace.

Within seconds, the mist cleared, and the hustle and bustle of Devonport filled my senses again, with that my grandmother groggily woke up. She became very ill that night, and for all her efforts regarding avoiding doctors and hospitals, she willingly accepted her fate and allowed herself to be admitted to hospital. Within little more than an hour, she had passed into a deep sleep, it was more like a coma because she didn't move or flinch whilst being attended to by the nurses.

With that, I was told to go home and wait to be informed. Now being a real Devonport maid, I do not appreciate people beating about the bush, if we had been in Devonport, I would've been told to "piss off back home, to grab something to eat and drink, then wait to be told that, "we'll give you a bell (phone) when she's about to Croke it!" … I could handle that.

But not the false sympathy that was showing in the doctor's eyes. I remember returning to her bedside to kiss her goodbye not a final kiss, but just the normal kiss goodbye that you give to people you love. I was just about to plant her smacker (Devonport for A friendly kiss) when the horror of my location hit me. Realising I'd left my bag at Grans house in the hassle of getting her into the ambulance.

I was suddenly snapped back into reality and normality of the situation. Where Gran was concerned, she always had a way of annoying as shit out of me in one way or another. In the days of no mobile phones, there was no chance of me contacting the Welshman or anybody else for that matter; I sat there like a plank after realising that I was probably going to have to walk the nine miles back home. At that point if she wasn't dying I could have honestly bloody killed her, for putting me in yet another sticky situation. Then I was hit with the realisation, that my Gran never went anywhere without her bag and it was the panic of grabbing her hand bag and purse and all the fuss of getting her complaining and moaning into the ambulance, was the real reason I had forgotten mine.

Then I remembered that she was in the habit of always keeping a few notes and change for the children. Me being of sensible practical Devonport stock, with no shame or guilt started to remove her purse from her hand bag. After all, I was in great need, and she wasn't going to need money where she was going was she? This justification went through my mind, plus she loved the bones of me did that woman. Overjoyed and relieved, I've been saved from a miserable wet 9 mile walk home, I bent down to kiss my gran goodbye, only for her eyes to flash wide open stare at me just like she did when I was a kid, like she always did when I'd been caught red handed up to something naughty.

And say these immortal words, words that I will never forget, "put my soddin purse down you, light fingered Cow!" Those were the last words she ever spoke to me... she died soon after. Blanche Victory Peace Hill, born 1919 named in celebration of the end of the First World War. Born in the Barbican Plymouth, my rock, my beloved grandmother, my biggest supporter passed into my history scolding me to the end.

This is a woman who couldn't tell a joke to save her life. However, there is hardly a story or a situation she was involved in that I can remember where she didn't end up being the cause of hysterical laughter. She always accused me of laughing, even if the "cats' ass was on fire", but I don't think anybody could have honestly kept a straight face around her. Her life and antics make me laugh to this day, her death and rising out of a coma just to call me a like fingered thief cracks me up!

However absolutely nothing tops her funeral! Her grand finale, resembling a mixture of the Benny Hill show and an extract from a keystone cops movie!

I should have said penultimate to her grand finale because trust me her burial was even worse! I'm laughing now so you will have to excuse me for a moment.

In Devonport we would say, she just cracks me up!

Chapter Seventeen

What could go wrong?

My darling grandmother had a brilliant way of dealing with grief and that was to completely ignore it, quoting "what the eyes don't see the heart don't grieve over". I've seen her coping mechanism many times throughout our time together. One episode that particularly stuck with me was the death of my mother at the age of 52 by cancer. I remember walking that short distance to my grans house, after receiving an almost hysterical phone call from my brother Joe, informing me that our mother had just died.

I clearly remember me pleading with him to give me at least an hour to calm my Gran down; informing him this news could possibly put her in hospital with the sudden shock of hearing such dreadful news of her daughter's demise. Then remembering my annoyance, when Joe informed me that it was too late, because he'd already talked to her. He defended himself by stating it was only right that Gran be informed first, seeing she was Shirley's mother. At the time, I don't remember feeling sad, or upset about the news just that I was angry at my brother! I was also deeply concerned for my grandmother's mental state,

Well to cut a long story short, I shouldn't have been worried. Gran seemed perfectly fine about the whole thing. No crying, in fact she seemed in complete control of herself, taking me back if I'm being honest. But knowing my Gran like I did, there's always some kind a catch. I remember taking in deep breaths while slowly climbing up the stairs to her house,

I can still feel the memory of my hand trembling knocking on her front door.

To my utter surprise, when she answered, she appeared to be perfectly fine and certainly nothing like a woman who had just been informed she'd just lost her only daughter. At the time, I thought the best thing for me to do was to just sit back and read the situation take my time and wait because you never know what's round the corner when someone, especially the elderly, goes into shock.

Even more especially, where my Granny Blanche was concerned! However, she was showing absolutely no sign of shock or trauma. It was at this point; her behaviour was scaring the living daylights out of me. In the end I was forced to ask, "are you all right Gran? ". What she said next almost knocked me off my feet, by informing me that she was absolutely fine. Her daughter Shirley was in London, and that's exactly where she was going to stay.

She said that their situation hadn't changed one bit, apart from the fact she's not going to be woken up in the middle of the night with anymore by the drunken rambling phone calls from my mother! A strong indicator that as long as she didn't address the situation of my mother's death, for all intents and purposes, my mum Shirley was still very much alive in my Grans eyes, now if that's not a coping mechanism, I don't know what is?

In fact, she was unnervingly calm, especially when she pointed to her sideboard saying, "Get my bankbook, get the money out, buy some flowers, then go get your brother, and bury your mother. I'll see you when it's over, and you get back". As far as my grandmother was concerned, that was the end of the conversation. I tried to meet a concerned eye

101

contact with her because I couldn't actually believe what I was witnessing. But she just wasn't having any of it; I could see her mind was set, and that she was for once in her awkward life completely in control.

So, I left her happily tuning in to her favourite radio station, and set off on the long journey to London to meet my brother and bury our mother, the delinquent, Shirley Boydell. Many years later, I remembered reading somewhere about a tribe's most sacred law about when a loved one dies, the dead person's name is forbidden to be ever mentioned again and their memory is put safely away for ever.

It took my Gran years to mention my mother's name again. However, I don't recall her ever looking at a photo of my mother. It was like she had a lock on her emotions. This is something I've only recently realised I do myself, because if you come into my house, I'm the same. You will never see a picture of the people I've loved most in my life hanging on my wall not even a small one.

I've stated that, I don't believe in the supernatural, I don't believe in life after death, or that my love ones neither watch over or walk beside me. I believe in science understanding the biological fact, they're dead.

"What the eyes, don't see the heart don't grieve over ".

To make the situation stressful, I was smack bang in the middle of moving house, apparently that's another high stress situation. By nature, I'm quite methodical. I like to put everything into boxes everything has to be the right box; everything needs a place to live. On this occasion I found myself literally throwing our belongings into boxes, most people will understand being tidy and methodical was the last thing on my mind. I'm a manager by profession and was putting all my efforts in to make sure Granny Blanche had the send-off she deserved.

Unlike a lot of old people, she still had lots of friends attending even her old school pal. Bobby Ball was coming, I went to bed with a feeling that I'd done her proud everything was in place and her affairs were in order. To keep myself busy, I was going to start clearing her house of all those memories. The very next day, my control freak personality was in overdrive, working kept my mind from wondering and also to stop me from becoming morbid. Morning has broken, was the lead hymn.

The food was prepared. The children were dressed respectfully and me, dressed, like a queen with my head held high lead the possession to the front of our house.

We had assembled to welcome the legend for the very last time. I remember looking at my children with pride every single one of them, even the baby was behaving themselves quietly waiting for their Granny to arrive. We waited, and we waited and we waited! Until I'd completely lost my composure, then in true Devonport style somebody voice piped up behind me, "where the bloody hell is she!?

Oh my God the funeral service was scheduled for 11 o'clock on the dot! it was now almost 11:20! My composure went, I could feel myself becoming hysterical, that was the last thing we needed. Then the children had started to play and fidget. All I could think of was where is my soddin Gran? People's voices became louder with someone shouting. This is bloody disgusting! Obviously directed at the undertaker. The horror of the situation had just dawned on me when my little boy started jumping up and down with excitement There she is, pointing to the top of the street about quarter of a mile away.

They had taken her to the wrong house after failing to adjust my new address on their records.

Obviously, they'd panicked when they realised the old address was completely empty, and then they started randomly searching the streets, taking my poor Gran for her very last joy ride! We took off on foot, chasing that funeral car as it went down, James Street, then down Mount Street, then down Clowence Street, and then up Chapel Street the fools.

Only stopping when my little boy Marc literally threw himself into the middle of the road, almost giving me a heart attack with the message "my mum said to take Gran right to the effin church!" I entered the church, not like a queen, but sweating buckets, with my once perfect hair stuck to my face, I was coughing, choking and grasping my sides because of the horrendous stitch I had developed. The children were completely dishevelled and crying, however the Welshman was absolutely furious, bellowing at the undertakers in a booming Welsh voice, you've made her late for her own bloody fun-e-ral boyo! Just as the organ had stuck up Morning has broken; I cried for hours. It was an absolute total disaster!

Once I composed myself and recovered from the ordeal, we all cried but this time with tears of laughter, remembering Gran once again, causing another hilarious debacle as usual, through no fault of her own.

Chapter Eighteen

Final Destination!

When alive, Blanche's favourite hobby was talking about her death. She would drone on for hours about her funeral. She stated categorically that she was not to be buried and was terrified at the thought of being alone six feet under as she called it. Being my Gran, she was not satisfied with just stating her wishes in a dignified manner, or even leaving written instructions, no my Gran had to resort to threats as well.

Her favourite was that if I didn't follow her instructions word for word, and stick her in a dark muddy hole she would come back and haunt me for the rest of my life, like the little spiteful cow she could be at times. I do not believe in the supernatural, and certainly don't believe that the afterlife gave permission to its new recruits, or the privilege of haunting and tormenting the living just because they can't get their own bloody way. However, I do understand guilt and having a guilty conscience for whatever reason can torment and eat you up for donkey's years.

Privately, I hated the fact that this legends mortal remains were burnt to bits. It tormented me to think that a woman who had been a massive part of my life was going to be eliminated for eternity. I needed a talisman I needed somewhere to go. I needed a grave or memorial a sacred place where I could show my appreciation so I could look after her in the afterlife. I started to think of where and how? I then had another one of my eureka moments.

Apart from me, the one person that she loved most in her life was her own mother, Elizabeth Hill. As mentioned, she was a chubby down-to-earth salt of the Earth. Mother of fourteen. My great grandmother, another legend etched in my memory. Even though I was only seven when she died, I remember her well. With that I decided to have Blanche's ashes buried or interred should I say with her own beloved mother, my Granny Hill. It took the Welshman ages to find my great grandmother's grave, and with the help of the record office her plot number was found.

I was overjoyed at the thought of being able to visit them both, to lay my tributes. I planned and fantasised about spending summer afternoons sharing my dreams and unconscious thoughts with my two dear departed grandmothers. I'm not religious, but I am spiritual. Me and the Welshman set off on a recon mission, eventually by mathematics found Granny Hills final resting place. I say by mathematics because the graves were not marked in any shape or form. All I could think of was my poor Granny Hill after having 14 children was the fact that not one of them could even be bothered to dip their hands in their pocket and provide her with a headstone. Poor Granny Hill was just a number on a grid map. Well not on my watch! And unconsciously I started to design a fitting mausoleum for them both.

What Lizzie wants, Lizzie gets, my Welshman set off to arrange the interment of Blanche's ashes in her mother's grave. Only to return red faced and furious that the cost was going to be almost £400, which was a small fortune in those days, plus the fact that the house move had almost financially cleared us out. Basically, we were skint. Gran would've called us being on the "bones of our ass", or the good old English saying of not having a pot to piss in!" I was beside myself once again; letting my temper get the better of me, resulting in me ending up in buckets of tears! My Welshman, being an engineer by trade cannot be bothered with the ifs, why's, or what's in this world, it's either broken, or it's not. He can either fix it, or he can't.

I don't think I've ever seen him so deep in thought, he doesn't like to analyse things too much or think outside of the box. So, I thought. At a young age, this man had taken on every single suitor of mine, after winning his prey, and then having to spend a lifetime trying to tame this bad tempered shrew. No, we had come this far, he was not going to let a small thing like officialdom and finance ruin it for me. I will bloody do it myself boomed his voice!

Do what?

The Plan was to first collect Grans ashes. The execution, the Welshman was going to dig the hole himself and sod the council's charges, and then the Welshman was going to respectfully inter my grandmother's ashes, saving us a fortune of £400! The outcome of his efforts a very happy wife hopefully bringing peace and normality back into his life. Well, that was his plan. Anyway, he spent that week working quietly away making a beautiful memorial cross out of our daughter's old wooden cot, I thought this was a fitting gesture considering the fact she absolutely adored our baby Freya. We went to the local engravers and had a beautiful brass plaque made to sit in the middle. With the words, "To our beautiful Gran" followed by the usual, we love and miss you tributes.

The Welshman's plan was primed and ready to go the only thing he had to do now was to wait for my grandmother's ashes to be released. To fill my days waiting, I designed and created a beautiful wreath made up of a mixture of pink Roses and white coronations. Blanches favourite flowers. Once again, that feeling that I'd done, her proud, entered my body, my sadness and anger of that utter disaster that was her funeral was fading in to the background and this time nothing, and I mean absolutely nothing could possibly go wrong?

Famous Last Words

But this is Blanche Hill we are talking about here! As you've gathered by now, my grandmother was a walking talking bundle of disaster. However, this time I knew it was final, the end of a beautiful friendship between a dysfunctional, unlucky accident prone woman and a little black girl nobody else on this planet wanted. The day hit me harder than I thought and I was dreading this final goodbye. If life had a pause button, I think I would've pressed it right there and then just leaving the whole thing in limbo.

This is where a lot of people would say but "I had to be strong". But not me, I had totally turned to jelly I just couldn't face it. But it had to be done. I had to do the right thing basically, crack on and get it bloody over with. I remember clutching my wreath of pink carnations secretly terrified at the thought of seeing someone who had been such a large part of my life reduced to nothing more than dust and ashes. My Welshman doesn't do sympathy, not that he's devoid of empathy he just doesn't know how to articulate it that's all.

I remember our car pulling up outside the funeral directors building, and Welsh saying I "won't be a minute sweetheart". Then I remember him walking solemnly back to the car. I was dreading seeing the Secret vessel that was carrying her mortal remains. I thought I'd better stand but I don't know why? A formality I suppose to receive this precious cargo. Only to be confronted with the Welshman lumbering back the biggest plastic tub you could imagine it resembled the boiled sweet jars from the old shops the ones that sold confectionery by the quarter when I was young,

In truth it was hideous and ugly, not only hideous and ugly. It was massive as well. Passing it over to me, I remember the Welsh man commenting that she'd never "weighed that heavy in her bloody life!" I don't know why I was surprised because everything that involved Blanche normally ended by going tits up! After 35 years of spending practically every day in her company, why oh why did I think that this day, this final day of our time together would be any different?

Regardless of everything, I had to fulfil the promise I'd quietly made to her regardless of this hideous container. After all, she was not going to be in residence inside it for much longer was she! To guarantee nothing could go wrong the day before the Welshman had pre-dug the hole where her ashes were to be buried. He carefully disguised it from grave yard maintenance by a little Posey of wild flowers. I was thinking that this horrible plastic box was the last disaster my Gran would suffer, before she was finally laid to rest. I comforted myself thinking this will all be over soon.

I knew she would be so happy sleeping alongside her darling mother. You could drive right into the graveyard then take a multitude of little paths to the individual rows the graves were on, some marked some not, but all tidy in neat little rows. The plan was, the Welsh man was going to neatly place Blanche into her final resting place, cover her up, and place my cross discreetly on Granny Hills grave. Remember it had to be done on the quiet because we had not paid the Graveyard £400, they wanted for the privilege of throwing a bit of ash on a bit of earth.

I patiently waited; I could see the Welshman on his knees quietly working away. At that moment I don't think I've ever admired anyone more than him that day. When we married, he made me a promise that he would do absolutely anything to make and keep me happy and here's the living proof I thought.

When you deeply love someone, you get to understand their body movements; they can convey to you their emotions without even saying a word. It was at this point, I noticed something strange and uncommon where the Welshman was concerned, as I was looking at him intensely crouching over the grave he was carefully taking great care by his actions to respectfully bury my Gran, what came next shocked me to the core because what he did next was very uncharacteristic of him because he started to sob, and I mean really sob, I could see him from behind with his head bent his body was literally vibrating.

Then I saw this great big man stand up turn around clutching his forehead with his filthy mud soaked hands that left streaks down his face, what I couldn't understand was, why was he just stood there looking at me with a gormless look on his face? He didn't beckon me, he just stood there? Silently mouthing, I'm sorry! I'm so bloody sorry? My dignified grief was swiftly, turning to anger, I thought shitting hell, what now! At the very last post, my final act of getting rid and immortalising, my tiny geriatric tormentor, yet another problem looks to have arisen.

I can remember storming up that little path taking the steps two at a time, I can remember the Welshman trying to block my way with his filthy hands and I can also vividly remember the site before my eyes! Remember, when I said, Welsh had sneaked into the graveyard the day before and dug a hole for the dignified interment of my grans ashes, what I failed to mention, was the fact, none of us believed her ashes would be the size of about six large bags of damn sugar, every single TV programme I've ever watched, the burial earns were dignified, very often a little silver cup , and that's exactly the size of the hole Welsh had prepared for, not the massive great tub we were presented with.

All that time I was sat in the car, the Welshman had been desperately trying to discreetly make the damn hole bigger! Without a spade he had resorted to digging with his bare hands, to tell the truth he was very lucky because if anybody had walked past. He probably would have found himself arrested on a charge of attempted bodysnatching or one of modern day grave robbing the fool!

The crying and sobbing was in fact him cracking up laughing over the severity of his situation. He admitted of that episode weeks later, that he didn't know whether to laugh or cry. In the end we left Grannies grave, looking like a bloody cow pat with an old lollipop stick sticking out the top of it, due to the fact, no matter what Welsh did, no matter how good of an engineer, he was, he could not get that damn cross to stand up straight! We didn't laugh about my beloved, grandmother's final debacle for a long time. However, when we finally did; we couldn't stop not even to this day.

Three weeks later, I walked past her house. But it wasn't her house anymore was it. After my final sterilisation, all remnants of Gran had gone. Her windows were lifeless and her tiny little garden had started to look shabby. Inside, the house looked grey and empty. She was gone forever and that was the final kick up the arse I needed, the prompt for me to get my skates on, especially if I wanted to move on to pastures new. But where?

I'd never lived anywhere apart from Devonport; I've never really questioned the subject before, only pondered with the idea. But now was my actual chance. I could always follow the Welshman back to the "home of his fathers".

However, one feature about the Welsh race it's glaringly obvious they are quite tribal. A Cardiff born Welshman would not be happy or welcome in the neighbouring town of Swansea. They see themselves as separate entities. Reading history books, tribalism appears to be one of the reasons Welsh failed to fight off the English, with its one king, one country, and were one united clan.

Unlike the Welsh who would have one king per borough. No, that would not do at all, even though my Welshman being the proud patriotic Welshman that he was he didn't appear to like much about the Welsh race at all.

We pondered on the idea of Lincolnshire, but that was far too flat. The Welshman like me was too used to rolling hills and mountains. We both loved the beaches with their granite shorelines and their crystal clear waters.

The idea of living on flat lands was out of the question. We both made the decision instead of going up, let's go down? Deciding between us Cornwall was a much better option for us all. I'd lived on the Devon and Cornwall border all my life, separating Plymouth from Cornwall it was only a small stretch of water. The river Tamar dividing the two counties. In fact, as a younger person I once swam the Tamar under the strict supervision of my local swimming club. Plus, the fact that I just couldn't bring myself to walk past her old house, without having a nervous breakdown, was the driving force for our move.

In truth I wasn't just moving away, I was running away from the memories of my time with Gran. My fellow Janner's would say her death was exactly the "kick up the arse" I needed, to get going. Our first move was the small village of Lachley, not too far over the Devon and Cornwall border, but we just as well had been on the dark side of the moon. From the minute we arrived it was an utter disaster. Not only were the villagers hostile, stuck-up and unfriendly, they were the most miserable bunch of people I have ever encountered in my entire life.

I had come from a place where friendliness was the order of the day, where people cared and helped each other, people who looked after people in their times of need. However, this lot would literally see you starve to death. I'm sure they wouldn't even piss up your leg if your ass was on fire. The straw that broke the camel's back was the day we received a poison pen letter, concerning a crime that had upset and was downgrading the whole village!

..... HATE MAIL.....

Devonport Maid

Dear new occupants of Solomon's cottage,

We the village are extremely upset and feel your arrival and behaviour is lowering the tone of our beautiful village. Therefore we are politely asking you to remove the tea towel that seems to have blown off your washing line.

Many thanks,

The residents of Latchley.

Being from Devonport, I couldn't help it, I literally pissed myself with laughter. Anybody else would describe it as I roared with laughter, but I on this occasion, I actually did let out a little bit of wee.

Resulted in me adding a few rotten old pairs of underpants and a dirty old dog blanket to the offending tea towel. Just to wind them up a bit more! However, the Welshman did not see the funny side of it and went into defensive mode he seemed primed twenty four seven for a fight. The Welsh also hold brooding and strong grudges. From what I've noticed, they fight on their own terms, rather than the normal acceptable rules of engagement, nice enough people; however, they can be lethal when crossed. My dear sweet, Welshman was no exception, and that got me worried. Me coming from a rough inner city Devonport Council estate this stupid letter was like water off a ducks back it didn't affect me at all.

However, my upbringing forbids me to strike first, even if I take a disliking to someone, in other words, Devonport people do not draw the first blood! My clan had a strict code of honour regarding confrontation. However, this is the best bit, when the gloves are off, that's when somebody else has thrown down the gauntlet, you'd better "get your skates on sharpish" meaning all hell is about to break loose, so get moving if you don't want a fight. If I'm being truthful, I was far too battle weary to be worried about a few small minded stuck up bigots that lived in this small Cornish land locked and unattractive village.

Like the Spartans, I'd been trained in the art of conflict since the day I was born, and knew these people were no match for me, but the Welshman's brooding temper frightened me. So, I decided to "box clever", and started taking everyone on day trips, so they thought. |However, for me, the trips were carefully constructed reconnaissance missions, I had to get the Welshman away from the disaster of our new home and fast.

I can remember to this day driving through the massive dark archway of trees that seemed to go on forever, I can remember vividly seeing the sunshine at the end of the tunnel. And at the end of that beautiful leafy tunnel that's when I saw the beautiful picture book village of Calstock for the very first time in my life. It was breath-taking, and thoroughly deserved its title of one of Britain's villages that is situated in an area of "outstanding natural beauty". It's sat before Roman times peacefully on the Cornish side of my beloved Tamar River. The tiny village hiding deep in the Tamar valley is looked over by an impressive, massive stone viaduct. It was there right there and then that I stuck my unconscious pin in the map, I could feel it in my bones I had just found us a home.

We were welcomed to the village within the first 10 minutes by an old man called Jan on our arrival; the people were warm, friendly, funny and extremely welcoming. It was like we had landed on a different planet regarding the difference between the people of Calstock and Latchly. I could tell the Welshman was relaxed and happy. Within a month and with a lot of luck we had moved in to a small minor's cottage, lock, stock and barrel The Welshman's mood improved immediately. Just like Devonport people.

The people of Calstock didn't care if you were rich or poor.

They also never stood on ceremony, deciding to just pop in night or day for no other reason than to just say hello. If a true Cornish man likes you, you will know immediately, if they don't, you will never know. Because like my Devonport clan, you will be just left in peace to get on with your life, with absolutely no interference from them. They have the same philosophy of, "If you don't bother me, I won't bother you" and a Live and let live attitude. Normally at this point in my story the listener starts to enquire how, two villages that are in such close proximity to each other, can be so different regarding its inhabitants?

The very same question I asked myself shortly after arriving in Calstock. I was matter-of-factly told by an old boy "they'd be from bloody London maid" a scenario, you'll see played out throughout Cornwall where outsiders, not only Londoners arrive believing they were better than everyone else, even the local inhabitants!

All because they'd been lucky enough to sell their grubby little flat in the smoke for an exorbitant price, enabling them wealthy enough to buy a large country cottage in Cornwall. Many arriving full of their own importance, carried along with their own delusions of grandeur. These people, these outsiders, know absolutely nothing about community spirit only concerning their selves with issues like, who's got the biggest rhododendron bush, or as in my case an untidy washing line.

They are known to complain relentlessly to the local council, complaints such as a cockerel keeps wakening me up in the mornings with its constant crowing, lol, or the church bells are annoying me! Even though the same church has been ringing its bells for hundreds of years, and the best one is complaining about the smell coming from a farmers field, "is making me sick and filling my house with a smell of poo", not even being able to understand that muckspreading is an important part needed when fertilising the very ground that feeds us all. The list is endless with these Invaders.

There's sort of an unwritten rule, when moving to the west country, an unwritten list of do's and don'ts, and that's don't worry about what anybody else is doing, don't worry about how much (money) other people have got, and never ever, show off your wealth, live and let live and most importantly, keep your beak (nose) out of other people's business! Follow these few very basic simple rules then you're almost guaranteed to live, a quiet and happy life.

After a speedy departure from the lifeless and inhospitable Latchley and all its fakeness, we soon settled into real Cornwall life at lightning speed. It was like a breath of fresh air, especially our new home in Calstock. However, I would advise anybody not to be taken in by the beautiful small village of Calstock, with its picture book exterior, we soon discovered that beneath the surface and I mean just a tiny bit under the surface are the people of Calstock, and the only way they could be described was a village full bat shit crazy eccentric's!

Not a combined eccentricity because each and every one of them were unique. Within the first week, the amount of diverse and outrageous characters we stumbled upon was immense, especially for such a small village.

This suited me down to the ground as I previously stated, I'm highly attracted to the oddballs in life and the people who are different from the rest of us. The good old British eccentric characters, I just find them fascinating and by far more interesting than your average person.

One of the first people we met was a Red Indian No not somebody dressed up as Red Indian, but an actual real Native American. Why and how he was living in this tiny Cornish village? I cannot remember now. One day a person sat down beside me in the local pub dressed exactly like the mad hatter from Alice in Wonderland story books, what surprised me most every single person in the pub treated them like it was perfectly normal. It was not just confined to the adults either because local children would pass me in the street casually and expertly riding unicycles dressed in funny hats. We'd come across old people who had their face painted a variety of colours and designs for no reason at all, if somebody just stopped dead on the spot and started dancing in the street or even in the local corner shop it seemed to be only me and the Welshman who took any notice!

The village was totally Bohemian, with musicians randomly playing music anywhere they pleased. There was a dear fellow called Mad-Andy, who was joined after a few months by another eccentric man also named Mad-Andy as well! He was appointed the most Unimaginative title of "Madder then Mad-Andy"

In other words, Mad Andy 2, I was told the number was important so everybody could tell the difference lol. There were people who sat on the Village green bench's just playing guitars, bagpipes, flutes, whistles and the drums just for fun. I must admit after a while the drums were driving me mad, because the damn bongos would go off at any moment of the night scaring the wits out of me and the cats!

As we walked along the streets of our new home, we met poets, performing artists of every description. All the time you would be dodging people practising their flame throwing, they were crazy exciting and dangerous, they were often taken to hospital with 3rd degree burns. We loved the people flying the most beautiful homemade kites, the fire kites, which light up the sky at night; they were a site to see. One of the most bizarre pleasurable instances was finding myself surrounded by six or seven Vikings yes, Vikings, not guys role-playing. These were genuine, Norwegian and Danish absolutely colossal men!

As in pure Cornish slang, "what happened was", that comes at the beginning of every story in Cornwall, and by the way, in this part of Cornwall many centuries ago they had defeated an invading English army with the help of their Viking cousins. Who in typical Viking style rowed their boat all the way from Scandinavia to Britain, only to then row all the way down the north side of England, and down the English Channel to Plymouth navigating the Tamar river all the way to Calstock, helping the Cornish to defeat their fellows in a battle at another area of outstanding beauty, a place called Kit Hill, two or three miles from Calstock..

The Vikings I encountered were descendants of the men who undertook that perilous journey to help the Cornish; I was smack bang in the middle of a re-enactment.

However, give them their due; these guys actually did row all the way, even though they did have the use of modern day navigational equipment. The only way I can describe arriving in Calstock, is it resembled Barnum's Circus most of the time. It was crazy, it was magical and it was all totally unique, 100% harmless. I never met anyone with a bad bone in their body. To this day I still haven't.

The years passed, and we assimilated without really knowing it. It was quite evident that our daughter was pure Calstock. She had adopted the exactly same attitude as every other person who lived most of their lives in Calstock. I don't know if she is by nature, a pure eccentric, favouring me rather her dad, or if it was her environment that was to blame! |For the first few years of coming into her teens, she wore a bowler hat, strange to the outside world, but perfectly normal for this environment.

Like most of her school friends, fashion was a dirty word. Modern life was boring to them they preferred literature, the arts, especially writing the arts became her life. The girls, as I mention, did not favour fashion. Like false eyelashes, they couldn't be bothered to dye their hair, or plastering on the make up like most teenage girls. They didn't need it and they knew it. For some reason, unblown to me, and I've tried to fathom it out many times, is why every single child who was brought up in Calstock talks exactly like they've got a plum in their mouth! I'm not exaggerating these kids sound like they've been brought up by the royal family. It's incredible because most of their parents are Cornish or Devonian and a few

Devonport Maid

others from up the line, but the kids all speak with the same uniformed accent, which makes them sound exceedingly posh, for some strange reason, it's only the girls I'm talking about.

The boys, however, adopted the surfer dude hippy look, every single; one of them had long flowing hair down to their buttocks, and did not adopt the posh accent. The boys all seemed to talk in the same West Country accent just like the rest of us. I can't go on and explain any further because it's bizarre? Maybe somebody will explain it to me one day because I can't work it out. The years rolled on I didn't need to be that highly observant to notice my Welsh man showing signs of interest in the Internet and computers in general. Home internet communication was just starting and like most people we saw it as a fad or a bit of fun, and certainly nothing like today where 99% of us can't even watch the television without it.

About that time i saw it ad in the local newspaper for "Internet, ready Home built computers for £50" Bargain! I'll have one! At the time, I was chuffed to bits knowing I had found the ultimate surprise for the Welsh-man on Valentine's Day. Thinking it's a far better gift than the normal bottles of Welsh whiskey I've been getting him lately. But what the hell was 1 1/2 gig I wondered? The new, but second hand computer was bought, and its massive great chunky monitor was mounted on a little desk taking pride of place in the corner of our front room.

After what seemed to be hours of Welsh plugging in wire after wire and going red in the face with frustration. Finally, the computer was up and was with a connected to the Internet. It's was only then did we look at each other both thinking the same of, what the hell are we supposed to do now? Sort of

121

thing. I remembered reading a newspaper article about friends being reunited just by logging onto the Internet site. After registering you apparently get connected with all your old school friends. Marvellous I thought, but all my old school friends were back in Devonport so didn't actually need a computer for that.

I thought I'll give that a go anyway saying "let's have a look", Welsh being the man of the house took charge and said who do you want? Like he could somehow materialise up Brad Pitt. My answer was simple, my brother, Joe please. With his two index fingers, Welsh tapped out my Joes name and pressed enter. Only for a tiny thumb size photograph who in all honesty could've been anybody had popped up. Alongside it was a job title of IT management consultant, currently working for Reuters International.

The first thing I thought was no that's absolutely not him. At the beginning of the Internet revolution, a job title like that was like equivalent to an astronaut. You were a bit special in other words a computer whiz kid! However, the more I looked at the photograph, trying to imagine 10 years on from our last meeting, the more it started to look like my brother Joe, a dignified smarter looking and far more serious version of Joe. However, it' still had his look about him? All the time the Welshman was looking at me, waiting for yay, or nay I suppose. My heart told me it was Joe, but my head was telling me that the job title made it impossible, but what to do?

The computer pioneers of the early days, the whiz kids were something else, practically all self-taught considering the there was no such thing as a university or college computer courses. It was them who went on to design the university courses we take now. It makes me laugh when young people say keep the old people away from technology. Because its people like my brother the guys of our age group that invented it, the fools! Lol

Another thing that made the thumbnail picture and name impossible to be my Joe was the fact, the last time I saw him he was on the maximum security wing of a prison. My darling Brother, yes however the little shit was still an armed robber. All night I played the scenario over and over in my mind and the next day I got Welsh to find the details again on friends reunited telling him that I needed a closer look. This time I took my time and I squinted and closed one eye, and took a step back from the computer, I wasn't sure? So I squinted and closed the other eye, then got right up close to the computer and I still wasn't bloody sure! It was him but it wasn't him if you get my meaning.

Nowadays, you just send a nudge or thumbs up in those days we were terrified that we may be infringing on somebody's privacy or even reported to the police for harassment. However, my message was sent.

Hi sorry to be a bother,

But I'm looking for my brother Joe. Blah blah blah. Lots of new and wonderful things have happened to me. I've left Devonport and I am now living in Cornwall. Me the Welsh-man and children are all fine.

Many thanks, Liz.

Call me naive but for some reason, believing no harm could come of it. I had put my phone number at the bottom of the message.

Can you imagine doing that now? Once again, Welsh pressed the enter button! AOL was 1p a minute in those days, so we did not linger terrified of a massive phone bill. I don't know how long it was that evening due to the fact I had no idea how the Internet worked? Thinking back, I probably thought it was like a letter only difference being it was electronic and once you posted a message to someone you had a wait for a message back like the time it would take a conventional letter.

Well, the phone rang. I picked it up, said hello and the voice at the other ones said it's me! Just like those ten bloody years, and all I get is it's me! I can't remember our conversation apart from there was a lot of oh my God, you never, and laughter, it's certainly didn't seem like 10 years had gone by. Joe was talking ten to the dozen and was as excitable as he ever was, which surprised me, because I truly thought the stint in prison would have totally destroyed him, all I remember him saying was, I've got something to tell you? I knew I wouldn't get the information there and then, because in typical Joe style he always made you wait for the juicy stuff, he said his goodbyes with a promise to talk the next day then he asked the impossible.

Can you post a picture of yourself? Excuse me we had only just learned how to turn the bloody thing on, never mind transferring a picture through a device through a telephone line into the computer and then to a bloody thing called cyberspace? Meaning that was a no dear brother, informing him that we would love one of him.

In the days with no mobile phones or digital cameras, they were around but only for the privileged few who had the money. After following Joe's instructions to turn the computer on and press download, then to do this and do that blah blah

blah, we then waited for what seemed to be an age, I finally did get to see his face? Yes, it was a little older, but goodness me what a fine, smart upstanding gentlemen. This new long lost and recently found brother had turned out to be! Then all went tits-up. Our new computer started to have a meltdown Welsh press this button that button he logged of and logged back on again he unplugged the damn thing and counted 10 seconds but still no response, it was broken.

The Welsh man was understandably livid. I actually started to feel sorry for the guy who had sold us this miracle of the modern age. But one thing I did know for sure it was about to be slung in the back of the car, and ceremoniously lobbed back to the person who sold us an obviously broken computer. Poor guy, I thought you're gonna get it tomorrow. Regardless it had done its job and well worth the £50 because I was delighted in finding my long lost brother. I went to bed with a big smile on my face that night.

Our relationship was back to normal faster than you could imagine. We just fitted right back in to the same slots we occupied all those years ago. He was, indeed, a computer, Whiz Kid or man I should say. Apparently, he showed an interest in computers and how they worked someone working in the prison service who also had an interest pushed the matter, enabling him to study for all the qualifications needed in those days for employment in the fledgling industry. If he could have got out of prison a year earlier and obviously got some funding, he would've been in direct competition with people like Bill Gates, but hey hoe, such is life.

He still managed to forge a very good career, travelling first class all around the world, helping companies to network and drive profits using computers. I won't go any further into the technicalities of his job. Considering the fact, I know so little I will probably end up talking double Dutch, all I can say he got in at the beginning, he was good at the job and it made himself a fine career with prospects out of it. Not bad for an ex criminal at all. It appeared to be that Joe was only driven by money, and he wasn't particular where it came from, so working to get it seemed to be no hardship for him. Plus, the fact he was super articulate, handsome, with a wicked sense of humour, got doors opened for him more than it would most people. We had wild parties, quiet holidays, Christmas holidays. Super lavish champagne and lobster dinners in posh expensive restaurants, the kids were well treated too all the latest toys and gadgets, and I was dressed like a queen, he was absolutely in his element splashing, "this time his very own", hard earned cash about. The family Christmas, in all its glory, was firmly back on the menu again.

Two Christmases I distinctly remember, The first being almost a disaster before it even started, it was like a scene from Ebenezer Scrooge, Joe had purchased the biggest most expensive turkey he could get his hands on, no joke. This thing was massive; he didn't give a second thought on how it was going to be cooked! Knowing full well all he had to do was sit back and wait for me to provide him with his goodies. The Welshman is an engineer and technician decided if we were going to safely cook that monstrosity as he called it, we would need to be cooking it overnight that way it would be thoroughly cooked, and allow for a respectable resting time. That Christmas Eve, I went balls out I was truly in overdrive trying to make sure everything was perfect. We had a load of people coming. I also found myself losing my temper having to wait on Joe, hand and bloody foot. If he came into my kitchen during preparation time once, he came into the kitchen, dozens of times each time, offering me various glasses of some kind of festive beverage. He was like taste this, try that, or have a drop of this, or what's your opinion of this one? He went on and on, yep, you've guessed it that was all I remember. Apparently, I was so paralytic.

A result of mixing his festive treats on an empty stomach.

I had to be put to bed, also I was the butt of everyone's jokes, saying, at least she'll be up early for Santa! Ha ha. That was all well and good however the one thing they had forgotten in their Christmas shenanigans was the fact I was preparing to cook the monstrosity of a Christmas bird overnight. Before I had to be unceremoniously carted it off to bed. The thought never even crossed their minds apparently, the last thing Joe said before he went to bed that night was, I can't wait to eat my Christmas dinner tomorrow! Ha bloody ha! 9:30 the next morning, I open my weary eyes, and my first thought was oh crap!

Moral of the story don't get your cook drunk. The Welsh man, who likes everything in order, and likes to cross every T and dot every I was livid, at me, at the kids, even our cat came into his firing line, but most of all he blamed himself. Joe, who had years of disappointment solemnly accepted his fate, of being probably the only person in the world who was not having a Christmas dinner that day, that's how hard done by he felt. I am a half glass full person, an optimist plus stubborn with the attitude of nothing gets the better of me! So, I struggled to lift and fought tooth and nail to get that bloody big fat bird in the oven.

The good news was Joe did have his Christmas dinner that day. However, we didn't get to sit down till about 10:30 Christmas night. The build-up was beautiful; it seemed to put everybody in a good mood. Everybody took turns in laying the table. Masses of candles were lit and Joe being Joe scattered expensive chocolates and confectionaries randomly over the table. We had, and still have a log burner that we loaded up with logs and left it open. The room felt magical, instead of the normal rush to get the food down our necks; we were totally relaxed, taking everything slow. It was perfect, perfection gained by a total mistake.

Every year that followed, we always had Christmas dinner by candlelight late Christmas evening, it became a family tradition and provided me with the most beautiful memories. The second Christmas, I remember we decided to do something different. Joe being a London city boy was not used to wide open spaces and was in awe at the size and ruggedness of our wild Cornish coastline. However, I found myself watching my kids at the beach far more than I ever watched my children say in a park, who were well taught from birth, how to identify the many hazards at the beach such as rip currents, tides, and especially how to save yourself if you actually ever did get caught in these dangerous waters.

It didn't take much to persuade everybody to do something different. This Christmas a unanimous decision was to stay in a beach cottage. Forget special occasions, forget, stressing yourself out buying presents forget, running yourself, ragged to make everything perfect because nothing is more perfect than being next to pure perfection, and that's the ocean. To Joes delight, he realised one thing the Cornish love, and that's dressing up as a pirate, in many Cornish towns you will find shops selling everything you will need to look like the handsome Jack Sparrow or any cast member from the Pirates of the Caribbean franchise. You could be a grungy, toothless, pirate, a sexy lady pirate, or the most popular, the handsome buccaneer pirate. Joe was like a kid in a sweet shop. He was literally in the costume shop taking hours to decide his outfit. Then his boots, and then his hat, and then what kind of a sword he was going to carry, and he went on, and on, buying more and more while the rest of us resigned ourselves to eating pasties on the seawall. After all, all you need is a bloody eyepatch, was the comment of my non-flamboyant Welsh man.

My brother then went on to spend copious amounts of money for our fancy dress party. He was arranging for us that night, one thing, the Welsh man was looking forward to, being a big man who likes this food. That night, we gorged on a salmon so big, I had to curl it round till its tail was touching its head just to get it to fit, inside a large roasting tin, we had lobsters scallops prawns, practically everything the Ocean could provide, and of course Joe was paying! No way on gods earth, could we have afforded all that luxury.

We were coping financially, but far from comfortable like most of the normal families living in the UK at the time. We managed to put together a decent pirate's costume. We bought a few bits and bobs and improvised the rest, but oh no not my Joe! Who had disappeared into his bedroom for what seemed to be hours, thinking back, I'd almost forgotten he was there with us until we heard what sounded like an official announcement? "I'm coming out now" all I could think of was what the bloody hell is he up to now! Lol Drumrolls, drumrolls again. I'm not going to beat around the bush, I'm just going to say it as it is, he looked ridiculous! A cross between Vivienne Westwood and Charles the first ... with an eyepatch! And with that we all burst out laughing I mean not just laughing, we had with regressed back in to the good old Devonport pissing ourselves laughing, the laugh you do when you let out a little bit of wee! Welsh was hysterical, and my girls were crying with that laughter all the time Joe was stood there with one hand on his hip, and his sword held high, grinning from ear to ear. He was in his element.

Next day was Christmas Day, so we did what all good Cornish pirates do and that's head for the beach. We built a massive bonfire and we cooked Christmas dinner, ham this time, on the beach and it's favourite soundtrack, of the crashing of its waves. He later confessed that outfit had cost him a whopping £400! I don't know why he even bothered; because it was a waste of time him bringing a suitcase. Reason being, he never once changed out of his pirate outfit, the whole holiday and no matter where we went, we were always accompanied by my pirate Brother!

Chapter Nineteen

It's nothing

I don't know if it's because we missed out on our childhood together, or the fact we were basically just plain childish by nature, the both of us have been described as having a wicked sense of humour by various different people. We've got different fathers, and I never remember my mother having a good sense of humour so it must've been just plain coincidence, and that we were very similar in personality, when it came down to being able to see the funny side of practically anything. Joe also would laugh if the cats-ass was on fire and enjoyed nothing more than rolling about in hysterical fits of laughter!

His career by now was in overdrive. He was headhunted by recruitment agencies left right and centre. He was beside himself when the offer came from ITV television station. He even turned down a higher paying job, the simple reason being he was positive he would be rubbing shoulders with the many famous celebrities who obviously frequented TV studios. He described the interview process as "being over in seconds" that they couldn't offer him the job fast enough! That was it. Much to the delight of my star studded daughter Freya, he started collecting autographs practically every day for her. Any of the cast of Doctor Who, were particularly welcome. She's still got the posters with the personal messages on her wall, but the biggest star in her life, at the time was her uncle Joe. He was a big man in the media as she put it.

Every so often Joe would just disappear into thin air, and then all of a sudden I'd received a garbled message on my answering machine crackling out messages such as I'm in India! I'm horse trekking across The Tibetan Mountains! I'm scuba diving in the Maldives! or I'm am eating bagels in New York!.. Yippee I'm driving the full length of route 66! Then came the disaster message, like I've crashed a motorbike in Thailand! I am in Dunkirk on way to see the War graves and lost my wallet! Or I'm drunk! I've broken my arm! I think I've been poisoned! |The best one, I thought it was female honestly! Doors were being opened, left right and centre for that boy.

He was riding higher and higher plus in the best form of his life. He hired celebrity personal trainers, visited celebrity hairdressers, all the time my dear brother was hiding the fact he was an ex jail bird and bank robber! Years later when the lightbulb, which is normally quite bright in my head, suddenly went off and I asked Joe a question that had never crossed my mind. "Don't they check you out for these jobs?" In those days, I think it was called the CRB; his answer was "yes they do". I asked, well how the bloody hell, did you manage get the job because you were hardly arrested for shoplifting, this is armed bank robbery we're talking about.

Twenty

Bad feelings

I remember all his messages that he left on my answering machine. But there is one I will never forget. It started with the usual it's me, followed by. I've got "a really bad back" being tall and gangly, Joe suffered with his back all his life doctors could never work it out. It was just down to one of those things, unlucky I suppose, but this time the pain was different. I interrogated him over the phone, the only answer I could get back was, it's different. Barking down the phone, "see a doctor", was the motivation he needed to book an appointment.

Apparently, the doctor said it's probably nothing, but I will book you in for a scan just to see what's going on. Well, maybe his old injury was making a re-occurrence. Joe was impatient, as ever decided to pay for a private scan at one of London's clinics. The doctors said they thought they could see a shadow and he needed to book an appointment with the NHS doctor to get it sorted out. Talk about a paradox, the reason he had booked the private scan was because the NHS had quite a long waiting list! He waited. He waited, and he waited all the time his pain was getting worse. The pain of not knowing amplified it. I'm an optimist, but I was starting to get worried. I was starting to get those feelings I get when something is about to go wrong and go wrong it did in a spectacular fashion, now my Joe Doesn't like to do things by halves it was always all or nothing with Joe.

After weeks as usual, I missed his phone call again, only to find the red light on my answering machine flashing. As usual. The first thing I got was an "it's me" Joe. Followed by in an almost excited voice, I've got lung cancer! Then the message ended. A few months before he had been elated, ITV had presented him with one of those new all singing and dancing blackberry mobile phones. The ones that look like little computers with the keyboard. Since the day he received it, it was glued to him and in a perverted sense of fun. I remember enjoying informing him that mobile phones don't work. In our village!

But in London, he had wall-to-wall reception, normally one's reaction to a message like I just received, would make you jump on the phone finding out the ins-and-outs the situation. However, not me. As a defence mechanism I tend to hide, ignore, and bury my head in the sand, by doing so all will be well. But it wasn't well, was it? It was far from bloody well. When I finally got the courage to speak to him. The news was even worse, I just couldn't believe, or hear what he was saying. But most of all, it was how he was saying it, there wasn't a bit of upset, shock or hysterical crying in his voice, it was just my playful excitable Joe! …

18 months max, they gave him and oh my God, didn't he milk it, he took the opportunity of his last 18 months on this earth to go balls out to "bloody enjoy myself" as he called it. I couldn't believe it, I actually couldn't believe my eyes, my ears, or make scenes of what I witnessing?

He systematically emptied every savings account he had, cashed in every ISA, premium bond and private pension! Later, admitting saving for his old age, pissed him off, and off he went on various adventures, pulling the sympathy card everywhere he went. He even got to drive one of those Californian, high-way police cars, a car he had always wanted. This attention seeker was the centre of attention, and was having the time of his life or end-of-life should I say! He also took tremendous risks scuba-dive. Pushing himself beyond what is considered safe, resulting in him on one occasion running completely out of oxygen. Luckily, an experienced diving guide buddy shared his tank to the surface. He was in his element!

The downside was he was hospitalised after every single trip, resulting in vicious arguments between the both of us. I normally go with the flow, but I could feel myself, this time losing patience. He's probably the only person I've ever known who actually looked forward to the chemotherapy. His explanation was, it will give me a bit more energy to do this, or that, or any of the other multitude of plans he had in his head. He was like condensing his old age into that last 18 months; he was victorious when the 18th month passed.

To me bizarrely, he seemed to enjoy every single bit of it. He seemed to have a buzz about him when he was talking about making his last will and testament, and how his personal treasures were to be divided out Between friends and family, but (the straw that broke the camel's back) for me when he rang almost in raptures the day, he had arranged his own funeral. Piss off, why don't you just Sod off! To this day I don't know where that came from. I suppose my only justification was, I was at my wits end, I was sick to the stomach with worry or the fact I'm just plain human.

And that's exactly what he did. We spent two of those precious months, in a desert of silence. My eldest daughter Tamsin had become the adult in the family. It was thanks to my eldest daughter our sibling conflicts were resolved. I apologised something I rarely do. Reason being, if I tell you to piss off and go away, I actually really mean it. But this time I knew time was against me. In typical Joe fashion, the very next day the phone rang with the usual "it's me" introduction, and 3-2-1, we were back in the room, like nothing had ever happened.

Me and London do not get on; to say I disliked that place is an absolute understatement! I hated it with every single sinew of my body, I despised the smell, I hated the traffic and most of all I detested its population, from my beginnings in Devonport to my current status in Cornwall, I value communication and openness above everything, in London I felt no connection to anyone where Joe would just breeze through the streets, pushing past people, jumping queues, hardly ever saying, thank you, and never once did I ever witness him engaged in small talk.

Even when we have nothing to say in the West Country, we still find it within ourselves to comment on the weather with the casual "it's bloody cold today?" Or God "in-it-hot?" comment for no other reason, other than to connect with another human being. In London I remember paying a compliment to a woman "that's a lovely coat, you're wearing "and she looked at me like I was a predatory insect!

Before pulling her collar tight around her neck and scurrying away, giving me a fearful backward glance... I wouldn't even have call it a week before Joe resorted back to using his, "cancer", as a magic wand, this time inviting me to his bachelor pad for a week of sibling together time. All I could think of was, you crafty sod! He knew that this time he had me over a barrel, and this time I couldn't refuse, and biting my tongue off I agreed. From that very first night, years ago, me and the Welsh man have hardly spent a night apart, it was never planned or discussed, it was just the way we were. We were like conjoined twins, joined at the hip, best mates, lovers and most of all companions.

Being separated was not normal for us, our strength and powers were noticeably diminished apart. Looking at the Welshman's face, as my bus departed, I remember thinking this was probably the only time in our 20-odd year relationship that I actually thought of him being small. Afterwards, I put it down to trauma, considering the fact 18 stone and being 6 foot in height could hardly be described as a small man in anybody's eyes. It was late August and absolutely boiling on that bus to make matters worse. The bloody thing broke down before we even got to Exeter. The air-conditioning was knackered and to top it all. I was sat next to a stinking Chemical toilet. I was livid with Joe; my mood was so bad if the cancer didn't kill him, I would have at that moment.

They say that foresight is a gift and looking back. I now realise that I was suffering tremendous unconscious stress, I didn't realise at the time, the magnitude of my feelings, yet another one of my Grannies favourite sayings "what the eyes don't see the heart, don't grieve over "and I definitely didn't see the effect that my brothers cancer was having on me.

I certainly couldn't have comprehended the affect it was having on my physical health as well as my mental fortitude. Anyone who's ever had any dealings with this disease will know it just doesn't destroy the person it destroys everything around you, it destroys careers, friendships your hopes dreams. It eats and rots its way through your very soul. Plus it's the biggest liar and deceiver on this planet. Leaving you to believe in hope bravery and most of all that you are valiantly coping. When all the time in reality, it's controlling and dictating each and every action and thought, you are nothing. Another one of my old Gran's favourite sayings, especially when we are met with an impossible situation was to "bend over, put your head between your legs and kiss your arse goodbye ". Because truthfully, in the end, there's absolutely nothing we can do about it! We are pawns in this game and have a 50/50 chance of winning or losing in the game of life and death.

My phone rang with the usual, "it's me". Telling me to just jump in a cab and he'll pay at the other end, I knew the taxi driver was taking me on a wild goose chase and the long way around to Edgeware Road, but hay hoe, I thought I'd just as well enjoy the detour considering I was not paying the bill. He looked thinner, a bit grey, but I put that down to the appalling, traffic fumes and air quality.

Apart from that Joe was his normal self. Everything was laid on; he'd already pre-ordered a takeaway lamb curry bought me a bottle of vodka and the absolute show of having his ice maker going 10 to the dozen. I was always jealous of his icemaker and he knew it! The best thing about London was you don't have to go far, especially where Joe's high-rise modern flat was built. It was on the side of a canal, man-made, I think?

There were rows of coffee shops and trendy eating houses. Full of London, high earners, all being ripped off, left right and centre. Come on eight quid for a cup of coffee is taking the piss! What made me laugh they seem to be pleased, almost bragging that they are paying this exorbitant prices, bloody fools the lot of them. His flat cost him a staggering half of £1 million and consisted of two rooms, one medium-size bedroom and a living room with a kitchen, Joe called it, the dining area. In truth I've been in bigger static caravans in Cornwall, but he was extremely proud of his home. It was also boiling hot with windows that would open a maximum of 3 inches I felt stifled and claustrophobic, he didn't even know his neighbours name! All the time I was thinking, if I was back in Cornwall, I would be sat in the garden warming myself around a wood fire, eating drinking and laughing with my Welsh man, yes, I was home sick already.

Poor Joe soon realised that no amount of money flashy lights or trendy establishments could compensate me for what I had left behind in the West Country. Joe seemed tired, so I decided to take the opportunity and have a long bath. At least he had hot running water. However, another complaint is I like to have the bathroom window slightly open pretty hard to do, considering the fact his bachelor pad bathroom didn't even have a window! What kind of a bathroom doesn't have a window to let the condensation out? No wonder they all end up, riddled in damp resulting in the city dweller, becoming even unhealthier.

Scuttling out of the bathroom, being extra careful not to slip and cautious not to wake Joe who was taking his afternoon nap. I noticed something out of the corner of my eye, something that I had seen only once before on the night before Granny Blanche's death, and that was the light. The experience of being that of an intruder, the overall feeling that I was once again, disturbing an important process. Like with our grandmother, was this the time they or whatever was coming to take him out our lives and on to the next plane of existence, if one exists, that is? Yes, just like Gran it was happening again, death was circling!

But from what I recall, it was exactly the same. Just like that, he woke up and the lights/presence disappeared, and normality, crept back into the room. Whatever it was, gone for now. The next couple of months were a mixture of hospitalisation, treatments and frustrations for my Joe. At the end of November, an invite came from America, two of his oldest friends and made it back out there in the I.T world, and this visit was to be first class all expenses paid by them as a Christmas present. In truth, it was probably the only way these people could say goodbye, considering the fact working conditions in the US can be so brutal and cutthroat.

Employees, have been known to be refused time off for their own parents funeral. Not being a big thinker, this thought never even entered his mind. Once again, he was centre of attention and elated. However, the disease had advanced so far. Any insurance quote was topping thousands of pounds. To be honest, I was relieved; thinking at the time a journey like that could probably finish him off long before the cancer could make its final finale. In typical Joe style the, it's me, telephone call left me reeling "I'll bloody well go without it and take my chance! "Leaving me in utter despair this time, I remember crying out loud to the Welsh man that he doesn't seem to give a crap about anybody but himself! Particularly me.

Trying to talk him out of being centre of attention, it would be like trying to stop the spring tide coming in. Knowing him like I did, I didn't even try. "Piss off to America, and don't come crying to me when you end up dead!" was my mind set. He was treated like a king. He enjoyed every moment of his visit. He'd waved his cancer, magic wand, and all his dreams had come true, basically he had the time of the life he had left. He fell seriously ill on the long flight home, and was blue, lighted right off the plane to hospital, where they immediately drained both lungs of apparently almost a litre of liquid, fluid and blood? I liaised with his London friends and sat for the next two weeks like a coiled spring, ready to jump into action the minute the call was made that he was on his last legs.

Do you know when we say I can't take any more, in truth it's a delusion because when you love someone you take everything over and over again. You just keep on going. Well in the end it came and it was not what I was expecting. It was the usual "it's me call" The sod had survived. Not only did he survive, he'd convinced the doctors to discharge him with enough morphine to sedate a herd of elephants.

Once again, he was back home, in his trendy little flat ordering luxuries of the Internet, left right and centre, no matter the cost! He had taken to video calling people any time of the night, knowing he would not be refused, after all who would refuse a dying friends call! My God, he was milking it even more. I took to wondering if I was the only one pissed off with him or was I the only one who was a just a mean bitch...

"It's me, I've booked myself into a private hospice Lizzie please come quick!" was the next message. My journey to London was a blur, unlike the last visit. I remember every single inconvenience, even the little things that annoyed me, but this time nothing. His lovely house was filthy, expensive cheese and patties were rotting in the fridge, on the kitchen side sat the biggest and most decadent cake I've ever seen untouched and uncovered.

Saint Mary's hospital is a modern clean building, built around an ancient Gothic chapel, I found out later. By this time I was in a mess my mind was racing. I was shaking so much. I worried that I may be directed right to the rehab ward when I asked for directions; I remember standing outside of his room drawing in breath to calm myself. The last thing I wanted Joe to see was me out of control, but inside out I was right of control my emotions were raging, at that moment, I was this close to losing it, as close as I've ever come to losing it before. But I should have bloody known it, instead of a dying man wrapped up to the neck in blankets; I was greeted with a light show! Yes, an actual light show, being in a hospital hospice on his last legs, dying of cancer, my Joe had decided to go out in style!

Chapter Twenty One

Goodbye

When I say, light show, I mean more like twinkling lights, fairy lights or stars, dancing fireflies in a canopy draped around his hospital bed. He looked bloody awful, gone was his beautiful, thick hair, and gone were those handsome chiselled cheekbones, but thankfully, what had not gone, was Joe. He was still very much in residence, I could still see the excitement behind his eyes, and before I could get a word out, he beckoned me to his hospital bedside locker, putting one finger to his mouth, indicating quietness and secrecy.

He was like a naughty boy, opening somebody else's Christmas present, curiosity had quickly driven away my sadness, then I had one of those why am I not surprised moments because inside the cabinet a half empty litre bottle of Jack Daniels, a crystal shot glass, four cannabis, joints, and a box of extremely expensive chocolates! Yep, Joe was definitely still with us.

I can't remember how many hours we sat looking out of the large window. I do remember thinking that it was strange that a hospice would have such a large window, especially on the ground floor? Worrying that privacy may have been an issue, but thinking back I think they were like one of those one-way mirrors that you see on the films, the kind that enabled the interrogator to watch your every movement, leaving you oblivious to the fact that you were being spied on.

For long periods, we sat, and said absolutely nothing to each other. Not that we were lost for words we just sat, I suppose what civilised people would call, quiet contemplation. Then all of a sudden out of the blue he looked up, looked at me straight in the eyes and said I "never thought I'd end up like this" to this day that statement still knocks me sideward, because up until that moment, it was probably the deepest most fundamental life affirming statement Joe has ever made.

My Taxi had arrived, I knew this would be the last time i would ever see my brother in this world again... What did I say? What did we say? What would you say? Me, I'll see you later! Joe, I'll give you a bell!

Over the next two days, he rapidly deteriorated, and after all that preparation, all his composure, and all that training, at the very last minute he had decided he was not ready and didn't want to die! My brother had changed his bloody mind! On his very last legs he managed to use his blackberry for the very last time and found the strength to call two of his most loyal friends. Who to my eternal gratitude, humoured, flattered and joked him out of this world, or I should have said our world…And he was dead. Bye Joe X

Chapter Twenty Two

After the Storm, Cold Rain

What did you feel? How did you act and how did you cope when you received that dreaded phone call, that one informing you that your love one had died? Well, I didn't feel, I didn't act in a certain way, and I certainly didn't have time to cope, not out of choice because everything of importance was taken out of my hands that day concerning, the news of Joes death The echo didn't even have time to travel from my ear to my brain before my brain was taken completely out of the equation.

All I remember was picking up the phone to hear. I'm very sorry Mrs B, blah blah blah but he passed half an hour ago! It would be four long months before I could even comprehend that dreaded phone call because within that split second of picking up that phone everything and I mean everything between heaven and earth exploded. The one thing that will never leave me is the noise at the time of the explosion and the intense buzzing sound.

I remember it was also very black. I remember the fragments of yellow light peering through the holes that the explosion had caused. In that darkness, most of all, I remember the Welshman's cries of desperation. I remember being very cold, I also vividly thinking... am I dead? My initial thought was the Welsh man must be dead as well, because there was no way on Gods earth, would he let another man rip my knickers off!

There is no way on gods earth with the Welshman willingly, stand back and watch my body violated... The Welshman must also be dead. I thought what a horrible bloody coincidence for my children to cope with, having found themselves with their mother, father and uncle all dead at the same bloody time!

But the pain in my body, head and vagina reminded me that I was very much alive, but unable to do a damn thing about it. I had no will, no strength, nothing! For the first time in my life, I was a nothing. We all know that shock can have a terrible effect on the human body, but this was not shock. This was not one of those coping mechanisms, the kind that removes you from your body onto another plane enabling you to escape the horrors. This was something else?

My initial conscious or unconscious thought, was that a lorry had just crashed through the side of my house. My thoughts grew more elaborate, thinking that we could be victims of a lightning strike, yes; 3000 Million volts from the heavens would do it. I found myself, even in that horrible state fantasising that by tomorrow, me and the Welsh man would be the most famous people on the Earth by dying of a meteor strike how cool!

My delirium carried on, and on, however my pain, turned into pleasure. I found myself enjoying the floating light feeling I was experiencing. Have you ever found yourself looking down on the clouds while sat in a window seat of a plane thinking I could just bounce up and down on those soft beautiful white clouds? Yep, dying was not so bad after all. Until, then came the voices asking me. . Do you know your name? Do you know where you are? How many fingers am I holding up? Elizabeth, Elizabeth, Lizzie, wake up!

321. The lights slowly came back on again, hazy at first, but they were most definitely on. But the pain I thought was the result of a tragic accident that had befallen my house was very much within me. In fact, pain is a bloody understatement because the actual pain was raging through my body. The one thing that wasn't a fantasy or bad dream was the intense pain in my groin after having five children; I knew my vagina had been violated in some fashion? I sensed the Welshman's presence, and quickly came to the conclusion that I could not have been raped. Simple explanation is he would not have been here whole, complete, or in one piece, if he had witnessed me harmed in such a fashion. More voices, more questions, and most importantly, more morphine! I was in fact, in the ICU unit of Plymouths General Hospital. The pain in my vagina was the result of an emergency catheter being fitted.

The burning in my groin that added to my pain was a surgeon's incision, having to insert a tube to carefully thread it through my main blood vessels all the way up to my brain. My brain, a thinker's brain, a crafty brain a Devonport Maids brain and the only bloody brain I had. When a Cornish man says (what- happened-was) sit down and prepare yourself for an epic yarn. What-happened-was! There was no tragic accident, no lightning strike definitely no meteor that hit me. What-happened-was, I'm so strong and the "I can cope with anything Lizzie" on hearing the first line of my brothers demise, my brain exploded into fragments and I had a massive stroke. There, I've said it! The word I've dreaded writing, as part of my story. Because if I don't say it, it's not real.

Sometimes strange things happen in the most ordinary, and obvious situations. Some people spend their lives, trying to find the answer. Me, I find myself occasionally, opening the door to find the answer. However, being the impatient entity that I am, my tendency is to leave the door ajar and just crack on with life. That first morning of lucidity, I put all my pride aside and welcomed the bed bath. I needed it, after all although I'd had a massive brain injury, there was absolutely nothing wrong with my smell receptors, so a bath of any description was desperately needed. I chatted to a woman in the next bed; I looked out of the window. I thought about my home and Calstock.

Most of all I thought about my Welsh man, all alone for the first time, I thought about my children, my cats, I thought anything and everything. I seemed to be on a mission to push one thing out of my mind, and that was the fact that I was paralysed from the waist down. I sensed it not long after I'd woken up. But in typical Lizzie fashion, I pushed it to one side and ignored it like I tend to do anything I find mentally overpowering. But paralysed, I was. All I could think of was what the bloody hell am going to do now and the thought of being pushed around in a wheelchair for the rest of my life pissed me right off. Then the light bulb came on, that was Nathan Pickett, an entity. I've not given a moment's thought to for years.

I got thinking if the detestable Nathan Pickett could manage to kill himself with only one arm, I surely would be able to achieve it with the two arms and hands, that seemed to still have good coordination, thinking he's not going to get the better of me, and if the detestable Nathan could take himself out of the equation so could I. I set my plan in action.

Me being a matter-of-fact down-to-earth sort of person, I could not be bothered with any romantic gestures, I planned that there was going to be no heartfelt farewell message of goodbye for my family, especially for Welsh. He of all people would not need a letter to tell him how much I was going to miss him or how sorry I was. The truth is, that inner me, the me that talks to me, was not at all sorry, I was being the usual me.

The selfish deep part of me the side that can be downright self-centred. Bloody stubborn bitch that I am. In other words, it was all about me, me me me me! My life my death!

Of course, my family were devastated my friends were sad and in shock, and for the first time in his life, the Welshman, in desperation, depression, or drink, posted his feelings on the dreaded Facebook, reading, … "I'm lost without my wing man "that was the most fundamental statement (in public), the Welshman has ever made. I've never told him, well until he reads this story, that it was his few assuming simple words, which stopped me in my tracks, putting the whole idea of me ending my life by a suicidal act, completely and utterly to bed. I'm the sort of give me an inch and I'll take a mile girl and remember vividly.

The first time I felt a twitch in my leg so I gave it a good old pinch, To my relief, my pinch hurt a little bit so I pinched it harder make it hurt a little bit more, I then gave it a good old poke with a pen a nurse had left at my bedside. Me, being me, and on a mission by the end of the day I managed to completely bruise my leg to the extent, the doctors thought I may have had blood clots in my leg as well, as everything else that was wrong with me. Obviously fearing more dreaded tests, I came clean and admitted to my experiments, only to be rewarded with the doctor sticking pins in my legs and feet to gauge my reaction. Ouch, ouch, ouch enough said. Recovery started with a mind over matter episode, I remember sitting in my wheelchair when a stern faced physiotherapist, who i had taken an instant dislike to, said these immortal words, now-stand-up! My first thought was to scream in good old Devonport fashion, can't you see I'm a bloody cripple, you twat! But, to my astonishment, probably down to my explosive temperament, I actually stood up on my own 2 feet for the first time in two months.

There had done it, and like the old ancient Chinese proverb. My journey of 1000 steps started with just one! It was about 12 months before I could successfully walk with a stick all the time, followed by Welsh acting like a praying mantis, ready to spring and catch me if I fell and another eight long years before I could walk any distance without the aid of a stick, that came about thanks to my eldest daughter, who one day stated "you don't bloody need the stick leave it!"

Those of you who have been affected, will know it's a long journey, It's a frustrating journey, you've become an utter pain in the ass to everybody around you. You feel sorry for yourself, but in my case, I most of all I feel sorry for everybody who loved me because they were powerless, it's only you, yourself who holds the power to push and push until you get that end result. My advice to anybody who finds themselves in the same situation is to never give up hope and stop feeling so bloody sorry for yourself.

Within five months, I was back home. But not without the use of deception. The hospital was still keeping a firm hold on me and my rehabilitation. However, after careful inspection from visiting physiotherapists and an army of social care workers, the NHS provide to people after such a dramatic life changing episode, there were consistent home visits, home inspections and consultations. In the end I was granted weekend leave. I was elated to see my cats again most of all, I was elated to be home, and that was from the Friday to the Monday. So they thought! It was like trying to get parole from prison. In fact, I think a prisoner would have had a better chance of escape at one point, I found myself accompanied by my eldest daughter in front of a panel of 12 professionals, all deciding if it was possible for "them" to let me home! One thing you learn on a council estate is to be crafty rather than angry. Smile rather than use profanity, use your manners emphasising your please and thank you Deception comes easy to those who need to survive and thrive in a rough environment, and that's what I did all the way through my interrogation. Yes sir, no sir three bags full sir thank you very much that blah blah blah. There was not a chance in hell I was going back once I was out of that door Friday morning. In fact, over the week prior to my release, I sent my belongings bit, by bit home.

I remember the nurses waving goodbye with a see you Monday Lizzie "not on your Nelly" was my unconscious reply. That was at the start of another chapter of my life, I spent the next few months tackling my emotions of Joes death. Something I couldn't do while I was recovering in the hospital, but in the privacy and solitude of my own habitat I slowly came to terms with my loss and in old Devonport fashion; I just cracked on with it. My dear Brother had left me the contents of his London pad plus all his paintings that he had acquired. As I've mentioned Joe had expensive tastes, and took to frequenting art galleries and auctions to this day. His beautiful paintings hang on my wall but that is exactly what they are beautiful paintings. I have absolutely no idea there worth and I have absolutely no intention of ever getting them valued. To me, they're just my Joes pictures. He had also left me 10 K, and all his expensive designer top of the range wristwatches, the children 5K and hundreds of people gifts to the value of one K just to have a nice meal and a drink on him. Lovely gestures from a truly lovely but naughty man.

Over the next 12 months, things started to settle back to normal. I was never going to run a marathon. However, I managed to get around, started cooking again, picked up a few of my old hobbies. What do you accept when you have no choice in the matter, but I was taught to pick myself up brush myself off and start all over again? Gran would say, "if you don't, at first succeed, try and try again!" We relax back into normality, trying to put the whole sorry mess behind us, sometimes days would go past without me thinking about Joe. Sometimes I found myself thinking about him most of the day.

The day I got that phone call I wasn't particularly thinking about anything. The TV was on, and the Welshman was taking a bath which was a diabolical in itself. Normal people and I said normal, I mean myself, we are able to just kick off our dirty rags nip in and out of the bath taking just a few minutes out of their day, however, for the Welshman, and it seemed to be a major exercise. The preparation alone seems to take ages. The bath itself seemed to take all day and the drying off period seems to take a lifetime, he made a real meal of it. It was an absolute palaver at bath time; the Welsh had everything but the duck.

Knowing my husband like I did I would completely put off doing anything of importance, knowing that, if I even dared to try and hurry him up, I'd be met, with nothing more than an angry mass of bubbles and steam... I remember being annoyed having my afternoon interrupted by the phone ringing interrupting my thoughts, only to find myself talking to a very well-spoken gentleman, asking personal questions about my relationship with my brother? I was just about to hang up, thinking it was some kind of a scam, when he informed me he was from ITV television company, he, then went on to offer his sincere condolences on the death of what he called, a valued and well-loved member of staff. All I could think of at that moment was, how nice and considerate of you however, it's been almost 18 bloody months! Before I could open my mouth to voice my opinions, he then went on to inform me that there were a number of insurance policies or schemes. I can't remember which now, that were unclaimed.

By this point, I was bloody lost I didn't have a clue what he was talking about. All I can think of was just spit it out man for God's sake! I remember saying well what does this all mean? His answer came out professional, but still left me in the dark. He was saying something like because these policies were of a certain kind? And were not subject to probate or any last will and testament of the deceased person, right was my answer, go on! When I finally got to the bottom of it, they basically needed a next of kin to pay out the said money that the company gives as a corporate compensation to the loved ones of a deceased employee, and seeing my Joe had no kids "that we know of?" It looked like I was in the firing line?

He then went on to demand my certificate probably to prove we share the same parents or parent, the delinquent Shirley Rose, in our case. Then i was told to leave it with him. Which I did. I just as well been talking Japanese with a regional accent to Welsh trying to explain word for word something I didn't actually really understand at all, so in a very down-to-earth way, I just said, I think I may be getting some money owed to Joe and left it at that. Have you ever been in the situation where you had to count every penny just to get a loaf of bread? Have you ever been in the situation where you had to hide from the rent man? Did you ever find yourself in the situation where you had to go cap in hand to a family member, begging for a loan till payday? Have you ever just gone without, resigning yourself to the underlying fact that you are absolutely brasic, skint poor as a church mouse, as my grandmother used to quote good old English, saying you didn't even have a "pot to piss in?"

Not so long ago, Poor people used to sell their pee! Apparently, it helped in the dyeing process of fabric? Without that said pot to carry your precious liquid, you became known as pot less or piss poor, hence the saying he "didn't have a pot to piss in" meaning you were extremely poor... well, trust me on a few occasions in my life, I've been worse! Then imagine being that poor when suddenly a cheque for a six figure sum falls through your letterbox? Put it this way, I couldn't even write the exact sum down on paper, but I do remember at the end, it said and the sum of 33p! I'm going to be perfectly honest with you here; I looked as cool as a cucumber. In truth, I couldn't take it all in and felt myself becoming dizzy. All I could think of was. Oh no, I'm not going to be one of these highly strung women who faint when they get a certain kind of news, so I just sat down, looking at the letter all the time the Welshman was practically, literally, physically bouncing off every wall in the house!

We were rich and didn't have to worry about money for the first time, in our married life! The next day Welsh took off to Exeter and bought a sports car, I took to Amazon shopping and bought myself a pretty black blouse for the grand sum of £9.99. The next day we went to look at a caravan, Welsh how much is that? The dealer, that will be £24,000 Sir, Welsh, I'll take it, dealer, how would you like to pay sir? Welsh, cash! We paid every bill. We threw money at all the kids; even the cats had new collars. I'm normally quite frugal with money.

However, on this occasion it was Joe's money and Joe loved spending. Joe loved being generous and Joe hated thinking about tomorrow, so we went on a spending spree! Welsh bought the cutest, little soft, top, yellow mini convertible. The plan was a undertake the classic European road trip, in the classic open top car only stopping to eat sleep and enjoy ourselves, combined with no money worries, living free without a care in the world! And that's exactly what we did....

Chapter Twenty Three

Young again!

Within a week, the house was secured and packed up neatly. Cat babysitters were employed. The little yellow convertible was packed to the rafters. A car refrigerator had taken pride of place in the small boot and most importantly, Welsh handed in his notice. I say that matter-of-factly, because in reality, he actually told them to stick their job where the sun doesn't shine! And off we went, it's a strange feeling not knowing where are you going to sleep that night, but we didn't let a small thing like finding a comfortable bed worry us.

The money gifted to us, seemed to take worry out of the equation. To be perfectly honest with you, the fact I had absolutely nothing to worry about started to cause me some anxiety. Can you believe I was actually worried that I didn't have anything to worry about, if that makes any sense? The ferry crossing from Plymouth to Roscoff, took about five hours. We even booked a cabin just to have the luxury of privacy; I found the temptation of the duty free shop with its glistening bottles of perfume irresistible. However, this is probably the first time in my entire life I was able to afford any item that took my eye. Ironically, I resisted everything enjoying every single bit of window shopping, not so for the Welsh man who has always detested shopping. We found ourselves standing side by side just gazing at the water, looking back at England was like looking into the past, remembering only the good times, putting the whole sorry mess behind us.

Six hours later, we rolled off the ferry, grinning like excited children. The Welshman paused for a second, looked at me and said right, where do you want to go? Surprise me, was my answer! We avoided large, corporate hotels, generic furniture and corporate meeting rooms; dressing for dinner has never been our cup of tea. We've always found fine-dining pretentious, and a waste of money. I remember a few occasions, the Welshman literally losing his mind over the fact we'd just paid, in his words "£25 for a bloody carrot. Our favourite way of eating is quite plain and un-pretentious, nutritious and in the Welsh man's case lots of it! Being from the coastal region of the West Country, Fish is always a favourite.

I don't mean pretty little faffy farmed restaurant fish, I mean a monster, that's been dragged, kicking and screaming from the deep, gutted, seasoned and slapped on a charcoal grill, all served up with some fresh salad and crusty bread smothered in thick real butter of course. The same goes for the meat dishes. My personal favourites are the cheaper cuts the kind you have to cook for hours and hours tenderising in their own juice's, all served up with fresh vegetables and homemade gravy, or sauces, depending on the nationality of your dish.

Most importantly, those of us from the West Country find the Cornish pasty irresistible. In fact, the Cornish pasty or a Devon pasty. It's like a red rag to a bull. The one thing you should not ever do is get into a debate over the Cornish pasty especially in the West Country. I've personally witnessed what could only be described as a start of World War three, over an insult regarding the Cornish pasty. One debate that rages throughout the land is the "pasty crimp" The curly piece of artwork that seals The edges of the pastry to make the perfect half circle, the conflict has raged on and on for as long as I can remember, whether a true pasty has the crimp on the top or the crimp on its side? in fact, the best advice I can give you is to say nothing you see the Cornish are a race of little words it's what's going on behind that quiet, sometimes blank exterior it's where all the important stuff is being systematically dealt with One thing you will never witness a Cornish man do is brag, especially where money is concerned? The best bit about Cornwall is you could be sitting next to a millionaire and never know it.

The Cornish attitude to money is, why buy a new pair of shoes, when I've already got a pair, or spend their money on new fancy gadgets when an old and trusted tool, has been doing the job sufficiently for donkeys years. Truth is, you will never see a Cornishman coming until it's too late. Best advice is to just eat your pasty like a Cornishman and that's quietly. We travelled down the length of France, and when I say length, it was more of a zig zag. Every so often we'd stop, veer off to the left go back up, turn towards the right and come all the way back down again! There was absolutely no order to our travels. We ate when we were hungry, and we slept when we were tired.

They say money can't bring you happiness. I found money gives you choice and it's the choices we make, that make us happy. Obviously travelling from England down south, the temperature has started to rise, and that completely put the kibosh on our soft top odyssey. The poor Welshman almost cooking to death with the soft top down, thankfully, for the first time in his life, he used sun cream. Having point blankly refused in the past, stating he didn't want to end up smelling like a woman full of perfume and sticky cream. Every morning, he gave in, taking my advice on how much to apply. After a week, my efforts had paid off.

Even he could see the benefits; he had developed a golden glow to his face and arms, which actually quite suited him. I've only ever seen my Welshman two colours, "pure Viking white" or angry, rolling the bed in agony sunburnt red. I noticed his hair was developing little blonde streaks combined with his new ray bans this was not looking like my old man at all. Without the worry of work, me, the kids, the cats, the weather, the bills, petrol prices and the state of the economy, I could see him transforming there and then into a new man, in front of my very eyes. It's a funny thing, peace of mind and the most liberating feeling when you have it. We continued travelling from little town to little town, staying in cheap bed and breakfasts and small hotels, our only entertainment of the day would be sat, looking out over the ocean as usual, never saying too much to each other just taking in the quiet atmosphere. If I had to sum up my trip in one word, it would be peace. That's all; no grand statement needed just peace.

Chapter Twenty Four

Little Yellow Hobo

Our day's turned into weeks, I'd noticed all these subtle changes in the Welsh-man, but not once did I ever consider turning around the magnifying glass, and scrutinising myself. Absolutely, no insult intended however, I had started to resemble an old hippie, my coffee coloured mix, race skin had turned a Sunkist dark ebony, my slick "frizz eased to death" topknot was replaced with auburn, tipped ringlets, held loosely together by a huge silk scrunchie, to my surprise, I noticed I'd had lost some weight, for the first time in years, no childhood, I looked natural.

The Welsh man, who never comments on physical appearance, left me gobsmacked when he said good! I prefer you that way; you don't need all that crap anyway! Let me tell you a little bit about my husband especially his attitude to women. He's probably the first progressive man I've ever met. A man that truly believes a woman is equal to a man, that the different skill sets, which the individual sexes possess, makes us a perfect Yin and Yang equals, two opposites needed to complete a sphere.

I'd given up years ago buying sexy underwear, hardly surprising when the only comments I'd get were "they are not going to keep you very warm in this weather!" Or those shoes are going to kill you after a mile or two. This is why I've never needed to worry whether my husband had a roving eye or not. One example, he was sitting minding his own business on a beach, in the small seaside resort of La Rochelle France.

When what only could be described as an absolute goddess appeared, she was utterly breath-taking. She decided to strip off down to the tiniest little, and I mean tiniest, what I would mockingly call a dental floss thong, right in front of him! there was no way on gods earth was I going to be able to compete with that vision of beauty, deciding to sit back and watch the experiment unfold.

You could almost hear the hubba hubba whooping sounds coming from the other. "Obviously British men" on the beach that day. But what happen next made me choke on my cherry aid, watching the Welshman's reaction was priceless. No joke, she was bending over pulling off her shorts with her perfect ass, positioned literally 2 feet in front of his eyes! And what did Welsh do? First, he lent to the left. Then he lent to the right, then, to my utter disbelief, he tutted loudly, complaining even louder that she was "blocking his bloody view!"

I was in absolute fits of laughter, especially when act two, started, this time it was with the slow removal of her bra revealing the best tits I've ever seen in my life, by now I had given up the will to live! I truthfully, I would have given my right arm look like that woman! All the time, thinking that I wished I had never eaten so much or gone to the gym more often.

I then got rudely snapped out of my daydream, because this time, all I could hear was a loud "hells bells" coming from the Welsh man. I thought that's it, he's cracked, go easy on him, because every man has his limit of temptation, only to find he had flown into a violent rage on the discovery of sand, in his cheese, and salami sandwich!

Don't get me wrong, as a husband he's been highly passionate making my hair curl on more than enough occasions. However, I have been strictly, seriously and absolutely warned. "Any mention of any bedroom shenanigans in, your book, I'm off! " And been told, you can add a big full stop to that as well!"

That means I've been really warned lol.

We travelled home with our emotions as clean as the proverbial babies bottom, every single corner of our souls had been scrubbed clean every single loose end had been tied up neatly. Insecurities had been hung out to dry, without a single tiny particle of doubt hiding under the carpet of our inner selves. Worries, had been fumigated, our whole existence had been sterilised cleansed dusted polished to a high degree and placed back on to the top shelf of our self-worth.

We had been mended.

The penultimate part of our journey was to travel the full length of the Pyrenees Mountains. We'd been so impressed with the sites that had greeted us up in those majestic mountains, so we decided to experience them from ground level. Starting our journey at Andalusia and travelling north inland to one of Spain's major ferry ports, Santander. Santander is quite metropolitan in my opinion, not Spanish enough for me. However, Santander is a functional town that has a commercial purpose with cars, lorries livestock and goods from all over the world, and passengers travelling to England arriving every day and night. Our trip across Spain, under the shadow of the Pyrenees Mountains was nothing more than breath-taking.

The sunset, turning everything touched by it a beautiful reddish orange colour. It was a lot cooler in the evening and for the first time we drove with the little yellow convertibles top down, I can still smell the hundreds if not, thousands of vineyards we drove past on that final day . We were snapped back into reality when the time came to book our passage home, practically every inch of the ferry had been sold out, I could tell by his walk that the Welshman was livid again!

Explaining to me that they had hardly anything left where cabins were concerned, unlike the passenger ferry from Plymouth to Roscoff France. The car ferry from Spain to Plymouth took a lot longer with the ferries, resembling small cruise ships. They had facilities, ranging from snack bars to à la cart, restaurants, cinemas, dance floors, stages, and swimming pools.

The crossing, if my memory serves me right, ranged from about 1 1/2 to 2 days. Understandably a comfortable place to rest your head was of the most important issue, especially at our age. I was trying to keep the situation and the Welshman as calm as possible. My suggestion was to find a hotel in Santander until the next schedule crossing, or to find out what they actually did have left. Once again Welsh stomped off. One thing I had noticed is the closer we got to Home the more his old grumpy self had started to re-emerge. Right, he said, staring at a piece of crumpled paper. They've only got a pokey, little, dark, inside cabin, with bloody bunkbeds left! Or a thing called The Commodore Suite? Holding up both of his hands in desperation. I thought about my brother, who would have had absolutely no confusion at all, when confronted with a dilemma like this, however, the Welshman had totally forgotten.

We still had tens of thousands of Joe's money left in the bank. Welsh was livid, handing over the almost £800 for our cabin, "just for one bloody night!" as far as I was concerned, it's exactly the sort of thing my decadent little brother would have, without a shadow of doubt done for him. That brought a smile to my face, Joe did love the best. It didn't take too long for me to realise the real reason for the Welshman's foul temper, unlike the Plymouth to France crossing which took you across the English Channel, a relatively calm, uneventful crossing, The Spain to Plymouth crossing travelled up through the Bay of Biscay. To land, dwellers like me it was just another body of water, to anyone who is ex-royal Navy or a sailor of any kind, the Bay of Biscay can be absolutely treacherous not some, but most of the time. It really is a body of water, not to be trifled with worst of all under estimated.

The one thing I wasn't happy with what is the hustle and bustle of the crowds of people embarking on the ship that day. The Welshman and I had been complete and utter loners very often talking to no one but each other for weeks on end, we avoided people like the plague quietly enjoying only each other's company, but this was manic with people pushing, people queueing, tempers, rising, some cases, I actually started to feel a bit panicky in those crowds. They were probably quite civilised. However, I was not happy and desperate. To close the door on the cabin Welsh had so reluctantly purchased.

Chapter Twenty Five

Never in a million years

For those of you who have walked with me on this journey from my first page to this one, please take my hand, so we can walk to the last pages together, as friends. Right, take a deep breath, straighten our backs, let's go. One day out of the blue just like that, the Welshman asks "did you ever hear back from any of your DNA matches". He just as well stuck a red hot needle down my fingernail, talk about touching a raw nerve! Apart from the one lady in London of West, Indian origin, and one woman who I had absolutely no DNA association with, and was only the manager of her families tree who was obviously and openly horrified, her husband could be related to a black person and told me in no uncertain terms. "We have absolutely no connection to Africa", in other words piss off even though, he had shown up as a second cousin once removed to me,

I was technically a DNA Billy, no mates! After my brother's death was, I destined to wonder this earth alone. Apart from the cousins, I already knew about in Portsmouth the children of granny Blanches two sons, Robert and Vernon Boydell, including my own children that was it.

To make matters worse I was the senior member of our small Society. Just like when I was a child, fantasies about my parentage, started welling around in my brain. I often find myself fantasising that my father must have been left totally devastated by the loss of his young wife (The delinquent, but redeemed, Shirley Rose) and their beautiful, tiny, delicate, and highly gifted daughter, in other words, me!

My daydreaming had started to get out of control. It had to have been with me perceiving myself, tiny or delicate for God sake! As you can gather by now, I'm anything, but delicate I've been described as hard as nails. With that, I don't agree as I still have empathy. However, one thing I do agree with is that I am "as tough as old boots" when it comes to self-preservation, or in defence of others I consider weaker than myself. insults and disappointments are like water off a ducks back to me it just runs off, I don't know if it's because I'm used to it or I've become desensitised to the hard crap life throws at us from time to time.

Maybe I'm just naturally fierce, a warrior. I was still reeling and still slightly embarrassed. I'd encouraged my daughter to waste her hard earned money on that stupid DNA test. Forcing the Welshman off the conversation he had shared body and soul with me all the years we've been together, however he knows full well when to stop and when I don't want to talk on the subject, what he did, next was quite out of character for Welsh instead of nattering on about the weather, food or television to my surprise, the Welsh man refused to end the conversation of my DNA results! Suggesting I take the damn test again!

Those of you familiar with the new DNA technology know full well that DNA does not lie, people do. Obviously, mistakes can be made by crossed, contamination, or mislabelling, and the possibility of mixing up your saliva sample with your pet dog who they now also provide DNA test for, imagine getting your test results back stating you were in fact a German Shepherd or worse a flat faced pug!

The new DNA technology is so advanced it can trace back your bloodline for thousands of years. Even organisations like the FBI are now crawling all over these DNA genealogy sites, asking for volunteers, very often with good results, reviving and solving decades old cold cases. It's so advanced that if you committed a serious crime today and left a tiny strand of DNA evidence like a small strand of hair, disregarded cigarette butt or chewing gum, pleased with yourself, thinking you've got away with it only for a second cousin once removed to be born 30 years in the future, remarkable to think that his DNA could lead them right back to you. ...

All this, I explained word for word to the Welshman, requesting to "now please leave it" Explaining I'll never find my father, maybe 30 years ago, but I'm far too old now. He is obviously dead. And if I had any sisters or brothers, they would have shown up explaining once again DNA is infallible it does not lie; I was going to put the whole sorry mess behind me and forget it. Like millions of others seeking the truth about their heritage, I had made one monumental mistake by assuming all DNA companies were the same and cross matched with each other. They don't.

I had taken my test with one of the main three testing companies are thinking that would be enough, and oh boy was I in for a shock? On reading that the DNA company I had taken my test with mostly concentrated on people of European heritage where the other main company, in fact, the leading DNA company concentrated on the American market it was then I had a lightbulb moment. In reality the little cogs started turning in my head.

There are an awful lot of black people of African origins in America. With that Welsh stating loudly, you've taken the wrong bloody one! It took him less than an hour to order me, a new DNA test from the rival company. However, the one thing these companies do all have in common is the fact you wait, you wait what seems to be a lifetime for the DNA test to arrive. You wait when it's taken its long trip to America, you wait when it's being processed, you wait for more procedures and then you wait for your bloody results. Considering the fact In many cases like myself, you've waited for decades one would think a few weeks more waiting for your results would be a piece of cake, in truth. It's the waiting for your final result is the absolute killer. ...

It was Friday the 13th 20/23 7:30 in the morning when I open my eyes, "Alexa, what time is it "that's how I know for certain, this was always the first thing on my agenda for the day. Second is running to the loo for a pee, never forgetting the click the switch on my electric kettle on the way, my plan of action is to make my first coffee of the day. I say first coffee, because I've been limiting myself to only one, at a push a maximum of two that's if I'm feeling naughty. No specific reason, I just like rules I suppose, sixth action of the day I jump, right back into bed again I'm the sort of person, no matter what time of the morning I have to get up something I have always hated by the way.

I still have to have that hour lie-in in bed. I adjust accordingly no matter how early I have to get up, where the Welshman hits the ground, running with eyes wide open, water splashed over his face followed by coffee, toast, and out the door, he goes all within 15 minutes. His explanation is he would just drop back off to sleep even at the thought of getting back into his comfortable warm bed.

However, I'm the complete opposite. Within that one hour I seem to accomplish a lot. Important day-to-day annoying little jobs, emails that I've been putting off get written, my food shopping ordered, news articles read, then more often than not the odd game of Clash of Clans. Yes, you heard me, right? Clash of Clans the on line war game, in fact it's my number one guilty pleasure. I love it because you can be completely anonymous. The only thing other players know about you is your gaming handle, for all you old people, the name you make up for yourself mine being Willow. In fact, you can be whoever you want to be. I started playing about 10 years ago, just for a bit of a laugh to help the Welshman who had just started online gaming. When I say gaming, it's not gambling. It's just playing a game for fun.

The object of the game is explained by its title. You join a clan and you fight other clans to win points and the more points you have further you go up to the leader board. However, the game is taken very seriously with some people spending incredible amounts of money, by adding new defences and weapons of war to their online profile. After a while, my joining for a bit of fun and a laugh turned out to be deadly serious and practically a part-time occupation.

After 2 1/2 years I found myself the top player, and number one in the UK for war stars! Yes, that's right, a little old grandmother from Cornwall had taken on and beaten all the young men/women of the United Kingdom at a war game specifically designed to engage targeting the technological modern generation. So, stick that in your pipe and smoke it you millennials and gen X generation! To put another feather in my cap. I've also been The UKs undefeated champion for the for the last seven years. So, suck that up, buttercups!

I think you've got a good idea concerning my morning routine by now. Next on the agenda were the emails, something I don't normally look forward to that's why they are usually left to the end of my morning office work, and there it was "Your Ancestry DNA results are ready". The first time I saw a message like this, I could hardly contain my excitement only to be met with disappointment, after disappointment, left with the realisation that I was indeed alone, as we say in the West Country, I'm a right, Billy, no mates.

However, the Welshman had paid for this second lot of DNA testing; I knew he would be asking questions as soon as he got back in from his first job of the morning. I followed the link seeing exactly the same as I did on the last DNA test; it was reading 40 odd percentages European mixed with different regions of Africa. However, this time there was not a lot of African? There was a high percentage of Scottish. I laughed out loud. In fact, I belly laughed. Me 17% Scottish! A descendant of two families Reid and Linton from a place called Banff Aberdeenshire?

They also give you an interactive map with regions coloured in, depending on the percentage of DNA from that region you have in your cells? Forgive me, it's all very scientific as you can tell I'm clearly not, but I will explain in layman's terms as best as I can.

The fact I could be even part Scottish intrigued me, this result had really grabbed my attention. I could imagine the Welsh man roaring on the floor in fits of laughter because one thing I would've bet my life on was the fact I didn't possess one, iota of Scottish blood in my veins. Remember me saying a family joke was that no Scotsman had ever been Lucky enough to get his bag pipes under my grannies table.

Well obviously, looking at the results, one obviously had. Well, well, well chuckling to myself I decided to scrutinise the map a bit more and lo and behold a tiny, I mean the tiniest of green dots appeared on the left hand side of my screen, catching my eye it was actually the size of a full stop. To the left of the green dot was the unmistakable shoreline of America? I had difficulty expanding the page on my not so new and slightly untrendy iPhone 8+ me with my eyes trying to identify the tiny green dot was absolutely impossible! And my hour lie in had passed, forcing me to abandon my ancestral research. Me Scottish lassy! LOL

Chapter Twenty Six

Thunderclap and Lightning OMG!

A nd It was that little green dot on the left hand side of my old iPhones cracked screen unbeknown to me at the time, was about to change my entire outlook on life, forcing me to evaluate challenge and rethink my past... Hundreds of sliding door scenarios danced through my mind, instead of living in the present or remembering the past it filled me with a scenario, well hundreds of different scenarios of "what if moments" ...

The Welshman was just as baffled as me on the discovery that I was, in fact a Jamaican and not African after all. The DNA test didn't only discover I was a Jamaican it also through a series of complicated algorithms managed to pinpoint my family origins to the St Ann's parish of Jamaica, and to where my family roots originated from. I was, in fact, Afro Caribbean, and not African like I'd always believed.

All I could get out of the Welshman was rubbish! Or this DNA test is turning out to be as useless as the last one! It had also managed to pinpoint my jockness down to a small area of Scotland called Banff making me think this may be right leaving my day, filled with WTF! Moments from the Welsh man who, by this point was totally obsessed with getting to the bottom of it? Started Throwing in hundreds of different scenarios, me being more pragmatic and practical at this moment started listing unconscious questions, stating to myself the obvious that if I was not African, how come my dad was Sudanese then?

I quickly found myself answering my own question. He either wasn't Sudanese or he wasn't your father! OMG! That lying little trollop, (The delinquent Shirley Rose) my biological mother had been obviously sleeping with more than one man! Making me the proverbial cuckoo in the nest it rocked me at the time, but absolutely nothing surprised me about that woman. However, revenge and retribution at this point in my life was long gone my wayward mother was dead, yet Another victim of the detestable dreaded cancer, however she got a better end than she deserved in my opinion.

Having been nursed so diligently and lovingly by my brother Joe, her only son who like me, she also neglected and ignored throughout his childhood. He devoted himself to the last 12 months of her life taken care of her, every whim and tantrum, putting aside his criminal light fingered past, my brother was a far better person than me, correction than most of us. Who would have probably abandoned a relative needing that level of care, to the dreaded and often inadequate care system? For the next 24 hours I found myself teased relentlessly, especially by the Welshman having replaced. Yes, with the Scottish, 'ock aye.

He also started singing the light-hearted "you take the high road, and I'll take the low road" song at every opportunity he got! Not only content with that, he added oh, I'm going to Jamaica, and don't worry about a thing every "little things gonna be alright now" all his piss taking songs became his bath time entertainment. I laughed, but truthfully inside, I was absolutely savage, as if it wasn't bad enough having an absent father that you knew little to nothing about, my life had now been replaced with a father. I absolutely knew nothing about, zero zilch, nada as we say in Devonport.

My father on paper was African, my biological or sperm donor was 100% from the West Indies in the Caribbean with a fair amount of Scottish blood in him to boot. This was proven, by yet another complicated and clever algorithm which separated the level of DNA we receive from each parent. My mother possessed, no Scottish DNA, my sperm donor or biological father seemed to have a Scottish white grandfather! From the said Banff in Scotland UK.

A Son of a sugar plantation owner you've got it. Yes, in Jamaica, it was even easier to find his name and the name of generations of my Scottish grandparents, or should I say clan?   I didn't know it at the time, but there is a thriving Scottish Jamaican society, who would I thought? My heritage was getting further and further away from Africa and the person who I thought was my respectable, highly educated Academic father Abdul

Leaving the million dollar question, who was the perpetrator? The one responsible for sweet talking the delinquent Shirley Rose's my dear mother's proverbial knickers off? Not that that would have been too bloody hard!

By now you must have realised that I am of a fairly grounded practical nature. The one thing that gets my heckles up is over complication, I like straight edges, clean and understandable dialogue. I despise people who beat about the bush and say 100 words when you only one is needed. Example is on many occasions I've sat and listened to a friend or relative blathering on for hours and hours about a situation only to witness their utter disappointment, when asking the "what would you do in my situation lizzie?" question after spending hours explaining their exhausting linguistic and emotional Marathon. What would I say? Just NO. Because very often the word no is all that's needed. However, to too many that tiny little word can seem highly offensive.in Devonport there's a saying "we don't piss about"

That's exactly how I found my emotions that day, no more of this stupid genealogy I was pissed off looking for a father, who obviously didn't give a shit if I lived or died.so sod him!

Chapter Twenty Seven

No rest for the wicked

My grandmother, who was not in the least a funny person, found herself in the centre of amusing situations. I don't consider myself as a particularly interesting person; however, I've myself more than often thrust into the centre of one of these interesting situations. By now, I was a laughing stock, especially when trying to tell the story that I was half Jamaican and half Cornish, then trying to explain, my Scottish and French heritage was making me feel bloody ridiculous,

The cherry on the cake came when my cousin Maria, the only child of my mother's younger brother uncle Bob announced that she'd completed the Boydell side of the family tree. Who were, wait for it, of Viking descent! Practically direct descendants of the Count of Anjou. All I could think have been what soddin now! When I look back, I shouldn't have been surprised considering the fact, the Boydells were mostly all extremely tall and fair, I really was the odd one out. In fact, I stood out like a sore thumb among my first cousins of my mother's elder brother, uncle Vern, who consisted of three boys and one beautiful willowy girl Kathy along with the new genealogist in the family Maria.

The stunning blond and extremely tall Pirelli model and only child of Uncle Robert, Blanche's youngest son.

I'm the eldest of Grans, 3 granddaughters. I really was, or should say I am, the runt of the litter, especially in between these two Viking beauties. My genealogical list was growing longer and longer, by adding Vikings to my heritage. I was feeling so much like a mongrel I almost started bloody barking! I'd decided right there and then it's been fun, but I'm going to put it all to bed and with that ground breaking decision, I'd prepared to abandon the search for my father, right into bed with it.

But It must've been the Cornish blood in me because the very first thing I did even before I had my morning coffee was to open the Ancestry app', even though on closing my eyes, the night before I was resolute to put the whole issue of my heritage to bed. Cornish miners of were revered around the world for their ability to get to the bottom of a hole. In my case my existence on this planet was a big, black dark hole, and the compulsion to dig just a little bit further, was obviously overriding my conscious decision to just leave it all buried in the past

Once again, my plain old nosy parker curiosity had got the better of me, again. I found myself once again, and perusing my heritage, still highly amused at being Scottish. Unconsciously, I started to imagine what clan and tartan I should identify with? Remembering my red and blue kilt held neatly together with a huge silver pin, for some reason, granny never called it by its correct name, only referring to it as my pleated skirt. This is probably down to the fact she seemed to dislike the Scot's with venom. I'm positive this was down to the fact her brother-in-law and true Highlander; Uncle Sam McDonald teased her relentlessly in their younger days.

She often referred to him as the "Scotch git!", and could never get it, that Uncle Sam was just a kind-hearted joker. I remember him as an extremely kind and funny man, but hayho, that was Grans Cornish blood at work. When a

Cornishman dislikes you you'll never know, that's what makes the Cornish race so dangerous when crossed. I found myself grinning at their past battles as I carried on perusing my DNA details only for me to realise, I'd completely and utterly ignored my DNA matches tab. I'd been so wrapped up and intrigued with my new heritage. I'd completely forgotten to have a look and see if, and I mean if, I had matched genetically with any long lost relatives.

By this time my bladder was bursting due to my curiosity, I had completely ignored my morning routine of a quick pee, coffee and back to bed, job done now let's see if I've got any more 8th cousins 6 time removed... Open Tab!

. ... W-T-F! ..... BLOODY HELL and GET THE #%%% OUT OF HERE! Seemed to fall out of my mouth! Leaving me for the first time in my life well and truly speechless!

Chapter Twenty Eight

The Interview

To be completely honest with you, I really didn't expect to see anything of importance. Looking back if I was to be completely honest with you and myself, I really didn't want to see anything of importance. After grabbing my coffee and jumping back into bed, I once again grabbed my phone, the app was still live. All I had to do was press the button, for some reason and we now know the reason why was because inwardly I was afraid, afraid that I may be opening Pandora's box of secrets best left buried,

My grandmother's words were ringing in my ears. Yes, I was still being haunted by that wise, old owl "don't go digging, because you may not like what you find", through force of habit I completely ignored her advice by pressing the DNA match button. My first reaction was "what the bloody hell has happened here!" For some reason, the phone had thrown up an old profile picture of me? My eyes not being As good as they used to be couldn't work the tiny thumbnail picture out?

I can usually pinpoint the exact time and location of a photograph I've had taken, I squinted as I held the phone at arm's length only then did I realise that the picture had my face, but it wasn't me. Oh, my God!!! Underneath it gave me three options of this doppelgänger. Her Centimorgan level was high 1.652, meaning it has been scientifically proved she was either my

- Grandmother/Granddaughter! = NO.

179

- Full niece/auntie! = NO
- Half sibling!!!! = OMG!

And there it was just like that, something I had wanted all my life, a sister I could hardly contain my excitement when I noticed the second thumbnail this time a chubby male Reading At almost 2000 cM.

- Grandfather/grandson! = NO
- Full nephew/uncle = NO
- Half sibling!!! = 2 x 2 OMG!

And just like that, I had another Brother…

Her bio read that Tina lived in Florida, USA, and that she was in her 50s, God she was a good looking girl, but I would say that because she looked just like me. A little more digging, (sorry Gran) I discovered my new half-brother was, in fact, her full sibling Pascal, residing in Panama South America.

These few revelations had literally blown my mind to tiny pieces. One minute I was completely and utterly sibling less, next minute, within a blink of the eye, I'm one of three! My mind and emotions felt like they were in a washing machine on fast spin. Only then it dawned on me that these two people had been fathered by the same man that had made me. A stranger that I had fantasised and dreamed of my entire life. For the first time in my existence i had a solid cast iron lead, a map and compass that led to Abdul, my biological father.

The answers that I had spent a lifetime desperately searching for were just one simple, click away. So what was I waiting for? "Press the damn button, Lizzie", some people say the old wives tales are there as a warning or life guide for us and not just useless pieces of tittle tattle. By this time, one old wife in particular, my grandmother Blanche, was literally barking, the order, Elizabeth "do not go digging, you may not like what you find ". To be blunt, shooting from the hip, like a true Devonport girl after all that digging I didn't like what I'd found, I didn't like it, at all!

The second day of my second DNA adventure revealed more shocking or should I say, surprising, genealogical revelations regarding my family roots. On the discovery of my real old Cornish heritage. Yes, that's right, I didn't have to delve too deeply to discover that I was also Cornish. By this point, the Welsh one was openly and understandably, pissing himself, laughing, claiming he was married to a real life, pirate of the Caribbean!

Tracing my maternal side back, only a few generations revealed that the delinquent Shirley Rose Boydell was, in fact, a direct descendant of the historic and distinguished Tremaine family. The Tremains, who in their glory days were a powerhouse in Cornwall, a family who were bestowed many honours and privileges on them by the crown. The family seat being the magnificent now named the lost Gardens of Heligan. But, this time my head was reeling, and my heritage seemed to be getting wilder and wilder! It brought to mind the scene from the early 80s Highlander movie, when the gorgeous Connor Mc-Craig, played by the equally gorgeous Christopher Lambert, A Frenchman, may I add, was asked by a police man, "Where are you from?" His answer, flashing that gorgeous smile, was lots of different places!

That's exactly how I felt; part of me has started to regret taking that damn second DNA test at least before all this started being African was sufficient and easy for others to understand.

But now how on earth was I going to explain? This debacle, I felt a little bit like everything and nothing all at the same time, and the thought of trying to explain my confusing heritage now was not something I was looking forward to. Add all this information to my mother's side. My grandfather was a direct descendant of the Boydells of Grappenhall, Cheshire. Whose family helped put William the Conqueror on the throne of England, and were granted many titles and favours. I started to feel like a first class upper class mongrel. "From lots of different places "

Within a split second of me, pressing that button, six decades of fantasy vanished as fast as a magician's bunny! Gone were my dreams, gone my father's Heritage? The mathematical genius Abdul had been replaced by Ronnie, a Jamaican immigrant. Don't get me wrong, I must sound like a right stuck up cow. That comment would have seen me absolutely ripped to pieces in Devonport, in other words being "brought down a peg or two!" Bragging and acting like you're better than other people was strictly forbidden.

It was up to the community to elevate you, not you! Doing it yourself gets you classed as a boastful, big head. However, inside, I was livid. I had been demoted from a would-be African Prince's daughter, to the product of an illegitimate knee trembler, probably up a back of a dark alleyway, to the spawn of a Windrush generation migrant worker, specifically targeted to undertake the jobs British people did not want to do, was a pretty bitter pill to have to swallow.

My entire existence relied on fantasy to wrap it all up into one sentence, I was right royally pissed off, soddin livid was an understatement! I was even more pissed off, when I eventually got to meet the family, when I say family; I mean to say Pascal, who had appointed himself chief spokesman, obviously seeing himself as the head of the family, me included by his attitude. Messages were exchanged, our father was this? Our grandparents in Jamaica were that then on and on, and on, he started with a quick hi and introduction from what I remember as a "full length interview," explaining to the Welshman later on that day.

I've never been a shy person; I could easily be described as an extrovert. I was a little nervous but not daunted when the offer of a video call was suggested by my new found Brother. I read between the lines in every situation, I don't know if it comes from generations of my West Country ancestors watching weather formations and observing darkening skies worried sick that the next storm could destroy or wash away their entire village.

But we West Country people have excellent observational skills, a sixth sense we unconsciously read symbols, we observe colours and smells we get that tingling at the back of the neck. Be very careful, because west country people will be watching every single movement and micro movement you make, it can prove fatal to underestimate one due to their smiling friendly faces often mistaken as simple minded persona, because more than often when you think you're screwing them technically they've already screwed you, trust me, they are as crafty as old Nick.

Try getting into a detailed conversation with one, you'll find that you have talked for hours, completely spilling the beans on your life, loves and good fortune, only later to realise you know absolutely nothing about the Plymouth or Cornishman you have been talking to. This is because most of all they listen with their gut! Very often not being able to explain in any other words, but "I've just got a feeling", very often it's the only explanation they will give. Oh boy, didn't I have that feeling? The feeling that the chubby charmer was not all he was cracked up to be. I was ready.

If Pascal's intention was to impress me with my new found heritage, the poor sod had failed at his first attempt by not setting the scene. When the camera opened, he was sat in an elevated position behind a desk, full of computers and important looking paperwork behind him on the wall. A multitude of musical instruments, mostly guitars across the walls. I could imagine going for a job interview in a theatrical institution or a theatre with the amount of bric-a-brac and artistic paraphernalia that surrounded him.

Intentionally or unintentionally, he had positioned the camera beneath him, giving him instant authority by looking down on me. From then on, it was all me, me, me, me, me! Moving onto, I, I, I, I ended up with wee, wee, wee wee, wee! My family this family, my family that! His grand finale being was, we have family high up and doing very well for themselves in the record and music industry… blah blah blah blah blah. In other words, nothing more than noise coming out of a hole in his chubby face! Smiling outwardly, inside all I could think of was why don't-you just shut the hell up!

When I was a little girl, one of the first lessons I was taught, was that "empty vessels make the most noise," to "listen and learn", to "engage your brain before you put your mouth in gear". He rabbeted on what seemed to be a millennium. The guy had completely exhausted himself by the time he stopped to take a breath, and probably only remembered I was there I was there when he realised the camera was on. I think it must have killed him to say "oh what about you?"

Remember when I explained that there is absolutely no need to use 100 words when you only need one, this is a perfect example with me answering his enquiry with "not much really". I could see the panic in his eyes. He had just exposed himself as nothing more than a waffling, big headed, chest thumping, bragger! Poor Pascal had fallen for the oldest Cornish Pirates trick of take everything giving nothing back, and that was it. I knew his family, his life story; anyway, it was all over social media, overflowing with his own self-importance.

Further investigation on my part, was to reveal that Pascal and his siblings were probably dragged up on an inner city council estate in London, just like me. However, with one difference, I was proud of where I'd come from, and that I was brought up by real people and taught valuable life lessons by my clan. That to just be yourself, along with the attitude if other people don't like you, it's their loss and "you can kiss my ass". We are steadfast in our likes and dislikes, and never take the middle ground we are either in or out.

I didn't have a father figure. I had hundreds of father figures and grandfather guidance. As far as he was concerned, I was nothing more than an illegitimate country bumpkin living in the ass end of Cornwall, whose husband was a lowly taxi driver.

In my opinion, that was enough information for him to get on with! Never telling him anything more than the basics, any more is just noise,

In fact, that my lowly taxi driving husband had a university degree in renewable energy and electrical engineering. He's also a qualified electrician and weapons engineer. However, considering the fact my new found brother was so engrossed in his self and the music industry, I suppose me spilling the beans that I was the owner of a prestigious Sony broadcasting academy award I got years ago for a play I co-wrote would have probably sent him into a total meltdown! I'd like to say I proud of that award but it's lost in the back of some dusty old cupboard somewhere.

"Never judge a book by its cover "and "No matter how good you think you are, there's always someone better" dear brother.

(Granny Blanche) 1919-1993.

With all this going on, I had completely forgotten about Tina, his sister, my new half-sister, who seemed to have disappeared off the face of the Earth. Pascal kept saying Tina will contact me, but she never did. In fact, after that first fateful meeting, I never heard from him, never mind her. My west country extrasensory perception was telling me that she was following strict orders to let the big Brother do all the talking seemed like he was the only person qualified to handle the situation.

I know you can't tell much from a photograph. However, I got the overall persona of a timid, quiet person and after the usual Facebook stalking; I managed to find a few pictures of her in normal day-to-day life. The pictures said to me that she was a normal mother of three boys. A normal suburban housewife, no flashy photographs or sexy pouting by her, she appeared to be just another normal human being.

Trolling through her family tree which was open for anyone to see on the DNA site. I saw to my shock that she or they, I should say, had three more siblings, one more female and two males, one sadly deceased at 15, making me now, one of six kids, all spawned by the Jamaican carpenter. There was one old faded picture of my Jamaican sperm donor, and that my friend was the first time I'd ever looked in to the eyes of my biological father. I felt nothing, zilch, nada! ...

Then came the desert of silence... I found myself highly entertained with the amount of Jamaican cousins I had inherited my father was from a big family and it was looking like I was related to practically the whole of Jamaica in one way or another. I also started entertaining myself by building my Cornish family tree which was getting more and more detailed. I wasn't only related to the prestigious Tremaine family I was a direct descendent with John Paul Tremaine of Minerva, being my fifth great grandfather Born 1770, the great name was lost when his daughter Mary, my fourth great grandmother married ..

After a little more research, I discovered it was the First World War that literally wiped the family off the face of the Earth, leaving their massive sprawling country estate and beautiful gardens to fall into disrepair. I remember watching the restoration of the lost Gardens of Heligan on the TV. In fact, it was the talk of Cornwall. Little did I know that this was my family's ancestral home? I believe the National Trust invested its time and money and now the gardens are back to their full glory, earning millions for the Cornish tourism industry. Jamaica could take a run and jump for all I care; I was Cornish and that would do me nicely! As we say in the West Country.

I was surprised how quickly I put the whole bloody mess behind me. However, that lasted about five minutes; I started wondering if there was actually more of Ray Bonaparte's offspring's hanging about than just me? His lost daughter, who had just popped up on a DNA testing site? Weighing up the facts after being asked by my new sibling if I had any information, it was glaringly obvious that he had not only just abandoned me. He was also responsible for abandoning an entire family of five children not long after my conception, the rat.

When looking back and filling in the gaps, I realised poor Pascal in between his bouts of relentless bragging, kept pumping me for information regarding the whereabouts of the slippery family fugitive, Roy Bonaparte. Scenarios danced around in my mind I imagined his dying son, a boy no more than a child crying out for his father, crying out for the one person who supposed to have been put on this earth to protect him. I imagined my poor half-brother was probably more let down than any of us, another one who was just thrown away and ignored by our so-called father.

Then I imagined my half siblings poor mother left alone, not only penniless miserable, and deeply unhappy. Also abandoned left totally alone, independently to bury her dead son, Roy Bonaparte's son. By this point in my life, instead of putting the whole debacle to bed, I was raging, savage, fuming as God is my witness, I could have rung his scrawny little neck and probably would have made a damn good job of it. Considering the fact, the weasel of a man was about half the size of me, I had let my imagination run riot the scenarios that danced around in my head had started to resemble a chapter from Charles Dickens, Oliver twist and it had to stop!

I was brought up to be easy going "to live and let live" and never to over react. However, on this occasion if that was my mother, if the dying boy had been my brother Joe, that slippery old Jamaican would have been dragged back, kicking and screaming to answer for his crimes, no messing about, after all, I'm a Devonport maid; we don't piss about when it comes to deserved retribution.

That's the good old Davenport/West country way of dealing with assholes. I needed to bring my emotions back on track. The man had been in my life, less than a week and my sunny nature, my "laugh if the cat's ass is on fire" attitude had turned to one of hate and revenge. I wanted to go back to my childhood, I wanted desperately to go back to being Abdul, The African mathematicians daughter and most of all, I wanted to not be related to my father the Jamaican "I can't keep it in my pants" Ray Bonaparte in any shape or form.

Next to pop up as a sibling match came Miranda, A school teacher, Jamaican born woman living in the USA, and guess what the first question she asked was do you know anything about my father? But I didn't think yes, I do, he's a dirty, rotten skunk was an appropriate answer for a first introduction, so carried on with the pleasantries. She asked about Tina and Pascal. I gave an honest answer. That I haven't spoken a word to Tina I was perfectly honest, telling her that I didn't quite take to Pascal I advised her to talk to him herself, realising it could possibly be me that was the problem and not Pascal.

I didn't want to ruin anything for her. In other words, I buttoned my lips and kept my mouth shut. About my real feelings regarding our first meeting. I was astonished when a few days later; she got back informing me that she didn't think much of him either saying she's probably not going to contact him in the future. Giving me the relief, of it's not me, it's you, scenario concerning my new found brother. She told me she had one sister and a brother, who were all born to slippery Ray Bonaparte in Jamaica, immigrating to London in the early to mid-60's However, by that time our dear father was already here literally inseminating anybody who was daft enough to have him, and with that I added three more siblings to my list! Leaving me seething with rage!

The next week my new sister, who I was starting to get on with very well, asked me if I'd like access to her family tree, I gratefully accepted the invitation. I've never been able to resist a good nose around in other people's business. The One thing that struck me was, her mother was absolutely ravishingly beautiful, my mother was also stunningly beautiful it started me wondering how the bloody hell did he manage to pull these beautiful women? Women who could obviously have their pick of the bunch?

I didn't know what Pierre's mother looked like, but obviously he had a taste for beautiful women… I decided to have another genealogy day with pen and paper in hand. I was all set to tackle my new sister's family tree, then for crying out loud was another one of his children popped up on the screen! This time it was a death certificate for a baby girl named Dahlia. Who died just before her first birthday? The poor little soul but plain as day in the parental section the name, Ray Bonaparte, aged 18 was written in a firm hand, jumped out of the screen at me I couldn't believe it, the Jamaican man whore had done it again!

She explained to me that this baby sister's existence was only discovered when she first started building her family tree a few years back … So Poor baby, Dahlia was added to his list! By now, we are looking at a serial, walking, talking sperm donor and notorious womaniser; we could probably add the world's biggest liar as well. I could hear my Gran commenting as she often did on the discovery of a serial womaniser "The dirty swine needs stringing up" on this occasion regarding my father, I couldn't agree more.

Slowly, a relationship built up between me and my sisters in America, with Miranda making the long journey over the big pond. Unfortunately, my other sister Pauline was terrified of flying which is a shame because they were both absolutely obsessed with the Poldark series set in my beloved Cornwall. I guess they never imagined in a million years, when watching the beautiful landscapes on that TV programme that their younger long lost sister Lizzie was sat on that very same beach made famous by their favourite program.

It's a very small world sometimes, and it makes me wonder if all these complicated sliding door situations we find ourselves in, are they really just lucky coincidences or is there something greater at work?

Everyone loved Miranda when she crossed the pond to the UK It must have been really unnerving for her to arrive here from a completely black African American culture to be met with the predominantly Viking white inhabitants of my Cornwall. If she was nervous, she didn't show it. However, there was absolutely no need to worry, she was welcomed with open arms and open hearts like many of the true Cornish possess, I remember A few local boys even climbed The flagpole outside of our local pub, just to make sure she could get a good picture of our national flag, which is the black and white cross of Saint Perrins, stating that nothing was a bother to make a visitor, who was friendly to them, may I add" feel welcome. I didn't even try to explain that the true Cornish are completely coloured blind when it comes to race.

Only one hiccup, I was going to say a small hiccup but it could've proved catastrophic if she was driving that day! "what happened was "(is said when a Cornishman is about to tell a tall or interesting story) my new found sister stated she had always wanted a pint whilst sat at the bar in an English pub, I chuckled to myself, thinking well, if that's all you want, you're gonna be easy to please sweetheart hahaha ..Famous last bloody words!

We entered the Rising Sun alehouse in the little village of Gunnislake Cornwall (P18 9BX) My sister was in awe at the stunning views over the Tamar Valley to a small mountain range called chimney rock. It's something I see every day and take absolutely no notice of. The pub itself is made mostly of wood and bare stone granite, absolutely no-frills. It's heated by a roaring log fire most of the year, since Covid they abandoned electric lighting, completely you drink by fire and candlelight if you don't like that, you can always drink in the daytime. It is what it is, the classic "like it or lump it" attitude of the West Country.

My hostess skills were in overdrive by now, my big sister had come all the way from America just to see me and have a pint of ale whilst sat at the bar in an English pub! And by God, was she going to get it! First things, first Sis "what's your poison?", I was paying absolutely no attention to the fact that there must've been a massive cultural distance between us. If there was and she felt it, bless her heart she never said a word and humoured me all the way. I repeated in a more civilised tone what beer do you want? I could see she wasn't too enthusiastic okay then, lager? Spirits? Gin, vodka martini glass of brandy? Whiskey, Sherry port rum, Bacardi, Hells Bells, I was running out of ideas!

Cider with that her eyes lit up, thank the maker for that. I was delighted a cider was going down a treat. Mission had been accomplished and another brownie point to me. After all I was seriously out to impress my newfound sister. Have you ever heard of the term "lost in translation?" Thinking back, I should've had more bloody sense, but I wasn't thinking was I. I was now number 5 of 10! And my family was growing exponentially!

I pride myself on being meticulous. I've been trained in the hospitality industry at degree level; to manage the comfort and safety of passengers and guests in large hotels, restaurants, and international cruise ships... So, why oh, why did I serve my tiny sister, one of Britain's strongest and most deadliest ciders!

An easy mistake, you may think if the person you had provided the drink for was British or even European. However, my new big, but tiny, sister had been living in America from a young teenager, to her apple cider was nothing more than a refreshing non-alcoholic beverage, what I had supplied, was Rattlers, one of Cornwall's, strongest ciders enough to knock a full grown 17 stone farm hand off his feet. To a tiny little almost tee totalling woman it could have proved fatal!! To add insult to injury on serving her with the deadly brew I started regressing back into my ladet days, gleefully chanting, "Come on girl, drinks up and get it down your neck in, one!" Hold on because it gets even worse, all on her tiny, empty, fragile, jet lagged, American, teetotal stomach! Id' got my new found sister what we call in The West Country (absolutely bladdered!) Yes, I am a terrible person!

Thankfully all was forgiven. My sister wasn't the first person to fall foul of West Country Scrumpy, and she definitely won't be the last. There's an old saying "you can choose your friends, but you can't choose your family". Unconsciously I had chosen sister Miranda as a friend.

After her departure, a blanket of calm descended on my emotions, in plain words, I wasn't constantly over analysing the situation I found myself in thoughts of my old mentor Val one of many wise old owl's from Devonport who had one answer for every distressing quandary I found myself in, and that was "everything is for a reason Liz" in other words, piss off, shut up and get on with it!

And that's exactly what I did; life in my household went back to normal. I neatly broke things down to the basics, and that was that I had half siblings from my biological father, just like millions, if not billions of other people who live on this planet. Meaning I was normal, well that's what I kept telling myself!

Me and the Welshman settled back into our old ways. He fully accepted and liked the fact he had a new sister-in-law more than anything. The Welshman liked diversity; he especially likes and is drawn to people from different cultures. So having a new found sister-in-law, who was born in Jamaica, partly raised in London and residing in America suited him fine. Gran used to say, variety is the spice of life, and he has admitted on more than one occasion that he could have never settle down with a traditional Welsh girl, reason being, they were not diverse enough for him, unless it was Shirley Bassey, of course, plus he would have been far too young and far too poor to be of any interest to that beautiful black Welsh diva.

Having to settle for me, a half Jamaican half Cornish, bat shit crazy firecracker that had a temper, Torpoint chicken! Knowing me like you should by now, you will understand my peace and contentment lasted all of about 10 days, when I found myself once again thinking about my first DNA discovery and my half-brother Pascal born in London residing now in Panama and most probably off a council estate just like me.

My curiosity got the better of me, even though I decided to let sleeping dogs lie. I couldn't resist stalking him on social media sites hitting the goldmine on YouTube. There I found literally dozens of videos of his lordship. In in our introduction video, I saw the only one side of Pascal, the side where he wanted to put his best foot forward. However, on social media, I saw the other side; I should say the true side of my new half sibling. It instantly hit me, the reason why I've not taken to him in the first instance, I've already mentioned I'd found him to be boastful. However, in his own videos, his opinion of himself appeared so high, he had practically elevated himself into orbit, to the extent, and one would imagine if he bent over, we would have seen sparks shooting out of his ass!

I found myself grinding my teeth just watching his self-promotion videos. Looking back, he had a decent enough voice, and played the guitar well, but there was something about him. I just didn't like the bloke. There I've said it, I just don't like him, reason being, he was not likable. Nowadays, I feel a tiny bit sorry for him, from the very start he'd been dealt the short straw where my affections were concerned.

I remember Joe laughing and joking that, "nobody puts baby in the Corner "when there was even a hint of me, being left out or ignored. No, I only had one brother, and he was dead and buried. Nothing on Gods earth could ever replace him and over my dead body, would I let anybody else ever replace him. I analysed my emotions coming to the conclusion, understanding the reason why I had seemingly closed the door on a new Brother but was perfectly happy to open the door wide to my new sisters Miranda and Pauline is that they had absolutely no contenders in my heart to contend with.

Chapter Twenty Nine

Like it or lump it

At the very beginning of this memoir, I talked about how writing one's feelings down could be a form of self-administered therapy, I personally stated I did not believe I needed therapy well, I would wouldn't I? My peers and the multitude of female wise old owls from my humble beginnings in Devonport would definitely disagree replacing needing therapy with "what that maid needs is a damn good kick up the arse!" Or a good old slapping around the ear! (If I was lucky)

With that, I like all the Devonport people would be expected to pull up my big girl pants, stop bloody whining and crack on with life. After all that good old-fashioned down to earth advice, if you still felt miserable, you would be expected to hide it, or be accused of the worst crime imaginable, and that was one of being so selfish, you could be accused of The unforgivable crime of "bringing everyone else down with you", that unforgivable crime could see you ostracised for good.

As you've gathered, where I come from big girls, don't cry, unless you're pissing yourself laughing that is. Hopefully the picture I've been painting of the women of Devonport is one of strength and independence all living and bound by and sticking to a strict code of ethics, rules handed down to them by their mothers, grandmothers and great grandmothers. Reading back over my descriptions, explanations, emotions and all my rantings and ravings there is one noticeable factor missing, there's hardly a mention of any male input in my upbringing probably because there wasn't any, it really didn't matter that I didn't have a father in my life.

You see in Devonport men had very little control. Not just of woman, but of anything, from what I remember of the men folk they kept their heads well down for an "easy life" as they called it. Walk into any house on a Friday tea time you would see the same picture painted over and over again, that being the pay packet placed neatly on the kitchen table low, and behold, if it had been opened! Skimming your pay packet being the biggest taboo or domestic crime a husband could be accused of.

Tea was normally always between 4 pm and 6 pm on a Friday it was always fish and chips, not because of any religious significance of the Christian fish on Friday, it was because the women would be far too busy dolling themselves up. Getting hair and make up nicely done for the week-end shenanigans of drinking and dancing in the local pub or social club. I remember vividly standing in that Friday evening queue at the local chippy, which was the children's job. If you were lucky, you were allowed to spend the change on sweets on your way home However, but here comes the paradox, something that always confused me because you were under strict instructions to collect the fish and chips and then come straight home with no stopping for anything, or else!

Kids were left to run riot on a Friday teatime, not only was school over for the week, your mothers/grandmothers were far too busy dolling themselves up to be even bothered to ask you to do horrible, mind numbing tasks, such as wash yourself/brush your teeth or comb your hair, which, in my case was impossible due to the fact my grandmother had absolutely no idea how to care or look after and maintain a black persons hair, often resulting in me walking around with a thick matted Afro.. Earning me, the nickname of golliwog!

That word alone these days can get you completely cancelled from society. It can get you fired from your job evicted from your house and in some cases taken to court yes punished by the laws of this great land. I recently read a news article of someone even being arrested and unceremoniously bundled into a police car just for having a golly wog in there front room window!

The doll, the poor golly is now classed as deeply offensive. However, deeply offensive to who? Not me I can tell you that for a start! In fact, I've still got mine, the one I was given on my second birthday. He sits proudly beside Edward, the teddy bear I was presented with on the day of my birth, my birthday bear. I can categorically state that I see, absolutely no resemblance between myself and a 10 inch stuffed toy, wearing striped pyjamas with cut up wool stuck unceremoniously on the top of his oversized, flat head! It's laughable.

This Friday night/weekend scenario was played out the length and breadth of Britain, not just my Devonport. In my entire life, I only ever remember one, maybe two fights id ever seen between men in Devonport, unlike the women who would be knocking seven bells of shit out of each other regularly, often once maybe twice a day but only once, did I ever see a man brave enough to step in and break a Devonport maids cat fight up,

The rest, being far too terrified of the consequences and retribution for even trying to intervene. Crikey, even thinking about it would be bad enough. Devonport was a strong matriarchal society governed by the World of women; it was their way, or the highway, and no in between. Hand on heart, honest to God, I swear by the Almighty, I never once witnessed an act of domestic abuse against a female, unfortunately, I can't say that about the men. Not that any man I've ever known would ever admit to it.

The best part of the weekend was a great old British tradition of Saturday morning pictures. Another invention that governed, working-class society. Like Thousands or should say hundreds of thousands of British children that attended Saturday morning pictures. In fact, we were like greyhounds racing out of the traps or horses chomping at the bit to get out of the house on a Saturday morning.

I still remember us kids battering the living daylights out of each other to be first on that bus to get to those pictures. It was like a form of state government babysitting. The men worked like dogs, early to bed and early to rise from Monday until Friday. On Friday, they were given a brown envelope containing a wad of cash. All these hard working men had to do was take the cash home hand it over to the wife, for this act of generosity some would say stupidity, you would receive a fish and chip supper, a night of excessive alcohol consumption, a dolled up inebriated wife. If you were really lucky the men" may get permission to get your leg over at the end of the night.

Plus, a lazy Saturday morning lie-in and yet another chance of getting the proverbial leg over again, all the time undisturbed and happy with the knowledge the kids are being well taken care of at Saturday morning pictures, perfect! Life was good! To me it was like a form of social engineering invented to keep the working class happy and contented enabling the wheels of industry to keep effortlessly turning.

If the British weekend rituals were designed by a higher power, it was a stroke of absolute genius! I loved Saturday morning pictures, Flash Gordon being my favourite. Even at that age, young age of about 10, I knew that his rocket was nothing more than a tin can with sparklers at the back that shot unceremoniously into the air, with what I could I work out to be nothing more than a few bits of wire or a catapult to make it look like it was flying. I knew Mr Ed; the talking horse was actually sucking a giant aniseed ball. I knew Skippy the Bush Kangaroo couldn't really talk, and wasn't actually saying a boy had fallen down the old mineshaft. I knew it was all make-believe, but I just didn't care. I was in heaven at those picture shows.

One of the proudest days of my childhood was being made a junior usherette. That was even better, meaning I've got in to Saturday morning pictures for free and could spend my pocket money on even more ice cream, it was pure heaven! Every single memory of those Saturday morning pictures is one of pure escapism, I loved it. The only downside of Saturday was the fact you didn't get any dinner other parts of the world and posh people call at lunch, but to many of us working class brits its dinner normally eaten, between 12 to 1:30 pm our tea-time. Is between four and 6:30 pm.

Now this is where it gets confusing, especially to our American friends across the pond, because the hot drink Tea doesn't actually have anything to do with a drink or a cup of tea, because tea time to us working class Brits is food, a meal that sets you up for the evening, the largest main meal of the day the meal you have you after a long or hard day's work.

Hopefully I've made myself clear to the fact on Saturdays. We did not get any dinner reason being and I quote my grandmother "you've been stuffing your face at pictures all day you can bloody well wait for your tea!" I remember telling her once when you're old, and I'm in charge, I'm gonna make you bloody well wait for your tea as well! Resulting in me getting the proverbial clip around the ear for my cheekiness. I didn't say a word to that effect again, lesson learned, never repeated.

After tea we were booted, unceremoniously back out on the streets to play. So, the parents could get ready for yet another night in the pub. This was called the Saturday night, and if you were really lucky one of your parents with stagger back home from the chippy and give you, the leftovers, absolutely sozzled with drink, often letting you stay up late. I was an opportunist, taking full advantage of granny Blanche's inebriated state to get extra pocket money and the promises of certain expensive toy. On many occasions, I can remember her, holding her head in the mornings whilst, battling the hangover from hell, saying did I that I really promise you all that? Yes, I would say with puppy dog eyes, yes I was a very bad child!

Years later, I found out that I'd used a method government spy's used to extract information and that's to make the target comfortable. Feed and get unsuspecting victim drunk. Granny Blanche had fallen for the oldest trick in the book on more than one occasion

The finale for the working-class of Devonport was the Sunday dinner time session. For those of you unfamiliar with Devonport slang, a session is another term for getting drunk out of your mind. A small session would leave you normally a bit tipsy the good-natured, happy drunk, a good session, saw you slightly unsteady on your feet and probably whibbling that means telling tall or funny stories when drunk.

A damn good or massive session would see you violently frothing at the mouth, paralytic in drink, most probably rolling in the gutter drunk, normally after you've been punched or sparked-out following an argument with someone less inebriated than yourself.

Sunday dinner time was the very last time my working-class peers had to enjoy themselves. Setting themselves up for the coming week of mind numbing drudgery and servitude, mostly in Plymouths Devonport's dock yard. On Sundays, I found myself dressed up to the nines, in a pretty dress, hat and patent shoes. Along with the rest of the children, I would be unceremoniously packed off to church in my (Sunday Best) However, unlike the rest of the kids rather than a kiss, I was packed-off with a severe finger pointing warning, and that was to "behave your bloody self" and most of all to watch my mouth!

I realise now that Granny Blanche was taking an enormous risk with her good name and reputation as a competent parent sending me to any place of authority on my own. Reason being I was an opinionated child, however unlike now I didn't have any control of what came out my mouth. I say mouth, but actually, it was my mind. If I thought something, it just came right out. I would open my trap at random, spilling my unconscious thoughts regarding any situation, spilling right out of that hole in my face, regardless of the consequences.

More than often Granny Blanche could be heard proclaiming loudly for anyone who would listen, that worrying about her Elizabeth (me) and my outrageous attitude was turning her hair grey and making her old before her time! By this time Granny Blanche was only in her late 40s. If she was looking for sympathy from the women of Devonport, she was sadly mistaken. I can remember being in earshot, listening to her being rebuffed being told, you brought it all on yourself bloody self-Blanche, you've ruined that girl! All Because she had indulged my every single whim, literally letting me get away with murder when in reality, telling her a damn good slap would keep me on the right track, telling her "you will live to regret it "on many occasions, I personally believe them to be right.

As an adult analysing the situation all this advice seemed like a fair comment considering who my actual mother was, that force of nature and juvenile delinquent the beautiful, totally untrustworthy and out of control Shirley Rose, born storming through life with her total disregard for any kind of authority, add that to her "kiss my ass attitude" I suppose it was a very fair comment, looking at it now they were definitely right. However final analysis is how did that tiny, bullied, half blind, timid little girl such as my grandmother manage to produce not one, but two blousy, "You can kiss my ass" extroverted rebels, like Elizabeth and Shirley-Rose? As Gran used to say God-only-knows?

And in a blink of an eye, just like that, it was Monday morning again! Back to the mind numbing grind until Thursday. In Devonport, like thousands of other working class estates Thursdays were normally darts and pool night. Individual teams of men and women playing together or individually sexed teams, all representing Devonport for the winners' cup. This tradition was played out the length and breadth of the United Kingdom. A few drinks were acceptable; however, drunkenness or getting steaming was frowned upon.

The British working week has gone on for as long as I can remember. Long before I was born, continuing right up to this day, the weekend is a British tradition, and I don't see it diminishing now or any time in the near future. I remember some time ago laughing my head off when reading an article regarding an American chief of police who came to the UK to observe how the British police dealt with drunkenness, when asked how his observational trip went? With this the poor exhausted police chief paused sucking in his breath to explain however the answer he gave almost knocked me off my feet in side-splitting laughter, he said by 11 o'clock on a Friday evening, in my honest opinion, with a look of pure desperation answered that the "whole of the UK were steaming drunk!" until Monday morning when they all go back to work! Ha ha ha!

My first thought was that's nothing mate you should see Devonport on Boxing Day! I have fond memories. Because boxing day in Devonport was known traditionally as "ladies day". I can assure you, none of us ever acted like a lady, we were not ladies anyway, we were Devonport maids Born and bred to hardship. A tribe of women a clan who had known each other since birth, every Devonport maid over a certain age was called Auntie as a mark of respect, trust me, we respected our elders or else! The consequences of not respecting the elder members of our community were severe in all those years, with hand on heart I can honestly say I never once saw an elder disrespected, if you valued your teeth, you wouldn't even think about it.

If an elder wanted a seat we stood up pronto, if an elder told you to shut your mouth, we shut up, and if an elder asked you for help we would roll up our sleeves undertaking the task without question, these were the unwritten rules that we all abided by, not out of fear, out of respect. Good manners were said to be hammered into us from the day we were born. You could break the rules if you wanted to, but I guarantee you it would only be once, you would never be able to break them again.

One of the roughest most violent areas of Plymouth named on the National news as (England's Beirut) was without doubt the safest place for the elderly to live. They were known as The Devonport royalty. I titled this book Davenport maid meaning girl chronicling my life, the people, and growing up in Devonport what I really should have said, I was Devonport made! Forged in what other people have described as hell, fashioned by each and every one of them. Looking back, without a shadow of doubt I probably wouldn't have stood a chance in hell of survival without them and was taught if you want respect, you bloody well earn it.

Chapter Thirty

Gran...again!

My Gran's life of disaster started long before I was born. In fact, it's because of her incompetence, or should I say extreme "bad luck" it's only by a chance of fate that I'm here and able to tell my story at all, One stand out incident that She absolutely refused to discuss was the day she almost killed the pair of us, and when I say kill, I mean death of the permanent kind!

In the late 50s early 60s, there were absolutely no blurred lines regarding where the two sexes were concerned, especially regarding my Gran's favourite hobby that being fashion. From the day she'd left school, and was old enough to earn her own money, she had invested every single penny she earned on new clothes. Like a lot of British women of the day, she had a tiny little hourglass frame especially in her younger days, telling me how she sometimes had to save for weeks sometimes months to be able to afford similar, but obviously the cheaper versions of her favourite Hollywood film stars attire.

I've got absolutely loads of pictures of her looking very smart in her little two-piece suits, that were always combined with a nice matching silk blouse underneath to set her outfits off. On her legs she always wore a pair of dark tanned silk stockings in reality, probably the cheaper version of the day called nylons. Leading us down to her feet where and leading me right to the culprit of my dice-with-death story.

The sometimes debilitating and often crippling "pointy toed stiletto heeled" shoe. You're probably thinking by now how the hell could her Granny's love of fashion accessories possibly have an impact on my survival and honest to God was the closest I've ever in my life-time been to death.

Well, what happened was! You're probably thinking get on with it and I was going to explain what happened next, but I've decided to tell you how I found out about what happened next, if that makes any sense?

Fast forward 20-odd years from my birth with me deciding to go out for some fun. I'd finished my usual getting ready for another night on the lash (getting drunk) and off partying till dawn in Plymouths notorious Union Street. My first port of call was always my Grans favourite hangout, the Ker Street social club (PL1 4EH) Plymouth.

It was a perfect starting point for my younger generation selling really cheap drinks, and the music was normally quite lively in the evenings.

I always enjoyed myself. This was down to the fact the old people like Granny Blanche only frequent the club in the daytime. They would normally pass out asleep in front of the TV in the evenings. It was a perfect symbiotic relationship between me and Gran because we would be like ships that pass in the night, she never saw me there through the day, and I never had to put up her at night, perfect!

It was in the Kerr Street club; us local girls would congregate. Joining together in a pack to have a bit of a laugh and the chance to get a little bit tipsy before we embarked on the serious business of clubbing.

None of us actually knew who would be going out on the town at night all that was needed was to do was just turn up and wait. Sort of Like a lucky dip of hell razing banshees. Thinking back it was just amazing way for meeting up with your mates; I was never disappointed with the night's bad girl contenders. On this particular night I sat at the bar, watching the girls drifting one by one and it pretty obvious who would be my companions or tag-team that night.

When assembled, my sisters in arms for that night consisted of my trusted side-kick of years Judi, obviously, her almost identical sister poor Gina who always got the blame for Judie's often bad behaviour, Big- Mandy who was built like a tank, Carol little the oldest and sensible mother of the group and Dallas-Dawn because of her love for outrageously large shoulder pads. Plus, me who at the time actually believed I resembled Dianna Ross! Lol.

Individually we could handle ourselves. However, this pack was a force to be reckoned with. Low, and, behold, any drunken sailor, who decided to get out of hand with any of us, because in those days the Devonport girls always fought as a team and trust me you did not want to be near any of them if it kicks-off

My favourite spot to occupy in the Kerr social club was also my grandmothers favourite patch that being a barstool that was situated at the end of the bar obviously my gran wasn't stupid. Because was a perfect vantage point, you had a good view of the door and who was coming in day or night.

I was downing my second drink of the night when I noticed the old man smiling at me out of the corner of my eye. It wasn't unusual that I didn't know him as many people, especially the older ones would travel from other parts of Devonport to the

Ker Street to catch up with old work mates, So I just politely smiled back as I've mentioned before Devonport does not do strangers, meaning if he was sat there in peace and unmolested, he obviously had some kind of connection to my area.

But for some reason he just wouldn't stop smiling at me? I could see by his posture. He wasn't drunk meaning he was after something. At that moment all I could think of was the dirty old sod was eyeing me up! Predators of any kind, don't last long in Devonport so when Judy piped up her usual, "what's that twat looking at"? In the old man's direction, I was not at all surprised. However, what did surprise me was that her statement caused him to burst out in fits of laughter, then to my horror for him to proclaim loudly.

The last time I saw Elizabeth (Me) she was red faced, stark naked, kicking and screaming with her bare ass lying across my lap! With that, I spat my lager and blackcurrant out of my mouth and right across the bloody bar! I was absolutely savage, so livid that the old git was tarnishing my good name, well as much of a good name I had left at that point. But hang on, that's not the point. I may have been a bit of a party girl, but I don't ever remember being that soddin desperate or that bloody drunk that I'd lower myself to bonk an old man, who to be perfectly honest, looked like he'd been dead for six soddin months!

No, I was not having that and up I got to attack. (Verbally) my first words being "Excuse-Me" that may sound very polite to an outsider, however, when a "Plymothion or Janner" rushes at you screaming the words excuse-me! That my friend (is the Janner war cry) and means you are probably going to get your head ripped off and your assailant is going to do their best to shit-down-your-wind-pipe!

In other words, you're in big-big do-do verbally or physically, but more than often BOTH!

I was prepared to defend my honour, and bounded across that bar, like Tigger! Only to be stopped in my tracks by another old guy, who had come in between the two of us. He also appeared to be highly amused. Laughing, he said "calm down Lizzie", with that he turned around saying to the old guy, why have you not told her? By this time my head was spinning, at that moment all I could think of was told me what?

What has this old guy not told me, I wondered? I've always been as sharp as a knife, and can think pretty fast on my feet, but for the life of me I couldn't work out what the hell was going on, or what connection I had to this old man who'd managed to had pissed me off so much regarding an incident from my past? It was then the obvious happened, and I literally barked the question TOLD-ME-WHAT?

By this time, practically everybody in the bar had their ears-peeled, in other words they were listening in anticipation. The one thing Devonport people love more than conflict is scandal! In fact, it's a popular greeting we give when meeting a long lost acquaintance. We never ask "how are you?" More than often, we were greeted with a toothy grin, and asked "what's the scandal!" A position I've avoided like the plague!

However, deep down in my heart, I knew my unlucky accident prone grandmother would be at the bottom of this debacle, in one way or another. From experience I just knew it! With that, the peacemaker said Bobby, if you don't tell her, I bloody well will! And for the next hour I sat there open mouthed humbled beyond belief and absolutely bloody gobsmacked after being force fed word by bloody word, the story of our first meeting. It shocked me to the core then and still gives me shudders to this day

Rewind 20-Odd years,

When Bobby was a relatively young man, he ended his day grafting as a cleaner in Plymouths (Devonport dock yard) by taking an early evening stroll. Hobby lots of people enjoyed, as the views over the Tamar River to Cornwall's Mount Edgcombe Country Park are absolutely stunning. Especially in sunny August, the month of my birth, in fact that particular day in August I was an infant of almost 4 weeks old.

The walk along Richmond Walk Bobby was a path over the Mutton Cove area of Devonport, along and above the three seawater swimming pools at Mount Wise It carries you, to the steps leading to the Scott of the Antarctic's massive and grand memorial built to commemorate the life, or should I say death of Captain Robert Falcon Scott, and his team's heroic effort to be the first expedition to reach the South Pole.

Past that and it's down a small path to what's locally known as Commando beach, which is a small rocky harbour. To finish this lovely little costal walk, you carry on walking for about 10 minutes and exit on the Devonport side of the Stonehouse Bridge. Once referred to by the locals as ape-penny-bridge, or in the Queens English Half Penny bridge, due to the fact, the toll for crossing from the small town of Devonport into Plymouth cost you one penny, that was before the 3 towns of Devonport, Stonehouse and old Plymouth merged together. The joining of the three small Devon towns made up what is known as todays modern metropolitan city of

Plymouth, my home. It was a beautiful walk and perfect evening for the young Bobbies stroll.

Fortunately, for me Bobby never completed his evening stroll that day.

With an amused look on his face, Bobby reminisced about leaving work that day, saying it was bloody hot, and that he couldn't wait to get out of that soddin place. He described his walk along the top of Mount Wise that day, he described walking past the boating pond, not that the pond ever saw a boat. It was just used for the younger children and babies; they have a splash about and play, seeing it was a shallow only about 1 1/2 feet deep.

He described passing over the top of the girl's pool, which was a large 50 meter swimming pool for the more experienced adult swimmers. Then remembered glancing over to the boy's pool, which was slightly bigger, and housed the diving boards and a large slide. The boys and the girls out door sea water pools were just names given years ago, and have absolutely nothing to do with sexual segregation. However, I couldn't tell you about the past, to us it was a name. Boys or girls? It made no difference.

By now my temper had gone, I was completely captivated by Bobby's story and desperate to learn about an incident from my past, that he'd been sworn to secrecy over. Obviously by my conniving grandmother Blanche, as I've explained west country people do not like blasting out the story to you, and in order to hear it and to get the full story, you have to wait and be patient, because they do not like to be rushed. Rush them, and you run the risk of them dropping the conversation, storming off and leaving you hanging. Before you get to the end you will have to go through the sometimes lengthy process of this side of the story, their side of the story, often finding somewhere in the middle, the truth!

In other words, if they feel they are being rushed, its game over. You've been warned, and understand that the payment for a Janner's story, is your patience, the more juicy the story, the more patient you have to be. Bobby continued with his story explaining about twenty minutes earlier, that my disaster movie of a grandmother had taken the exactly same route as Bobby.

However, she decided to travel along the bottom of Mount Wise, on the same level as the swimming pool, as she would have past the boating pond at the bottom like Bobby travelled along the top to girl's swimming pool. The boys and girls pools were only separated by about five or six feet. And easy to jump from one pool to another.

It was when Bobby reached the deep end of the boy's pool, he said he was gazing out over Plymouth Sound when he heard splash! Bobby said "what happened was", I stopped for a fag, looking down at the boys pool and saw Blanche go ass over tit into the deep end! She was screaming her frigging head off. When they were dragging her wet ass out of the pool and were trying to calm her down, but she wasn't having none of it he went on to say that's when I saw what all the fuss was about.

By now, I was getting a good idea of where the story was going, only for Bobby to confirm that Blanche was carrying me at the time of her mess up, or should I say near disaster! That's right you've got it, my silly old, petrified of water and non-swimming grandmother, had fallen ass-over-tit into the deep end of boys swimming pool! If that wasn't bad enough she was carrying a precious tiny bundle, another words the three weeks old me! All I could think of was bloody hell Gran, ha-ha, not that I was actually laughing at the time.

Looking back, I often wonder how the hell we manage to survive.

Come on, who in this world would think it, was a good idea to carry a practically new-born baby on the edge of an 8 foot deep, swimming pool, wearing ridiculously high 5 1/2 inch stiletto heeled shoes? My Granny Blanche, of course. Bobby's story panned out like a movie being played in technicolour on the big screen.

However, in truth, I don't know why I was surprised. This kind of scenario concerning my grandmothers many mishaps have been a common occurrence running through out my life. To this day Bobby' story proved to be one of the most dramatic in the history of me, and the terribly unlucky Blanche. But no one noticed me, only Blanche and Bobby knew!

What the rescuers had failed to notice was that my grandmother was carrying a tiny bundle, which was me was wrapped up in a beautiful white shawl. No baby carriers for us in those days, we were wrapped up and presented to the world in the most beautiful handmade baby shawls. Mine was made of pure lamb's wool, meaning one thing; I literally sank right to the bottom of the pool, leaving my Gran paralysed with terror. However, that's exactly all her rescuers could see, and that's somebody who obviously couldn't swim who was panicking and screaming at the top of their voice for help.

Those of you who are familiar with water know that in sunlight at sea level all you see is the glistening surface. However, underneath the surface everything what lays beneath is practically invisible, especially a small child dressed in white!

Lucky for me, Bobby was situated high above on the walkway and saw everything that was taking place in real time.

He recounted to me that he knew he only had seconds to react, knowing no one would hear or take any notice of him, considering the pandemonium my Grans near drowning had caused. His description of my rescue was, "I jumped those friggin stairs, two at a soddin time!" By this time, Bobby was so animated he was stood up, waving his arms about going through the actions of his heroic actions, step by step, of his rescue of me that day.

Me, well I just sat there with an open mouth, with yet another one of my-oh, my God Gran what have you done now moments lol. With all my Grandmothers screaming and carrying on, understandably, a crowd of gathered and were now watching a tiny babies rescue in real time. Apparently, after I was dragged out, people were proclaiming I was a goner! By this time, my poor Blanche was bellowing and being held down probably to save her from even more heartache, of witnessing my dead body, pretty dramatic stuff even for my Grans standards.

Bobby literally downed the pint of velvet stout id just bought him in one, like with every bit of drama that happened in Devonport a small crowd had started to gather. I could see he was enjoying the attention, so I let him carry on. It was true, I wasn't breathing. Rightly or wrongly, Bobby held me upside down by my ankles, and slapped the living daylights out of my back and that brought me back to life! Well, that's debatable? And we will never know for sure, will we?

At this point, my Gran was quiet and prostrate, due to deep shock. The local women took over, helping Bobby to remove my wet, sodden baby clothes, hence his statement of me being bare ass naked lying across his lap. Was in fact the truth the-whole-truth and nothing-but-the-truth!

Since that day, every single member of my community kept quiet over the incident of my dice with death. Apparently, even a slight hint of the memory was enough to set my grandmother off into fits of hysterical crying that lasted for hours, meaning the whole community buried it and left it alone, until Bobby came face-to-face with me over 20-Odd years later. Bless him.

THANK YOU BOBBY X.

Chapter Thirty One

Friendship

My first friend in this world was Jilly Cusack. The daughter of a Royal Naval diver, "uncle Scouse and his wife, Gwenny". A kind, hard-working respectable family that lived directly beneath our flat in Pembroke Street. My second friend on this planet was a girl called (Judi) Judith Belinda Bromley. The daughter of a single parent barmaid known as Pat. Last, but not least, was Stella Moyssi, AKA (fluffy tights) the daughter of a Greek Cypriot immigrant father and his British timid downtrodden wife, Dot.

Let me give you a brief description of my three childhood friends. Jilly was a beautiful child, with long, black, poker straight hair. Her clothes were always immaculate. She was a well brought up child, who had impeccable manners. She was kind, intelligent, and extremely diligent. Granny Blanche couldn't have picked a better playmate for me if she had planned it, Jilly was the perfect example of how a little girl should be, and in other words Jilly Cusack was just plain perfect.

My other two childhood friends were known as Judy, the Jew and Stella, the Greek. Unfortunately, these two were far from perfect and absolutely nothing like my first friend Jilly. In fact, they were so far away from Jilly; they both just as well have been born on Pluto the furthest mini planet in our solar system.

These two girls went on to shape my life in more ways than I could never imagine.

Judi was ridiculously tall for her age. An extremely thin girl, at the time her hair was cropped into a boy's short back and sides. She had an extremely long nose, earning her, the wicked nickname of Judy, the Jew. She was kind to animals, but that was it, as far as Judy was concerned her fellow man could take a run and jump. Finally, Stella the Greek. A tiny delicate pale looking child with masses of unkempt out of control curly blonde hair. Her face being as pretty as a picture, she was extremely funny, talkative, but highly deceptive, and lethal when crossed.

At five years old, I broke away from my wholesome, playmate Jilly joining forces with a girl gang known locally in Devonport, as "Judy the Jew, Stella the Greek and Black Lizzie".. To put it plainly, we were monsters! In reality, we were oddballs. Each and every one of us missing something in our young lives, that something we eventually found in each other.

And so, it began the original "girl gang" long before it became a popular term used in the national newspapers, when describing out of control council estate girls. It all began in the mid-60s, in the playground of the local school "Mount Wise Primary", when I first noticed the tiny blonde Stella prostrate flat on the floor sobbing her little heart out. Me, not being able to resist drama, found myself drawn to the situation, especially when I noticed the most ignorant uncaring girl in the school, focusing her attention on Stella as well.

Even more interesting was the fact Stella was clutching a Matchbox, not a tiny Matchbox that every smoker carried in their pocket at the time, but the big Swan Vesta type that were used to spark up our open fires and gas cookers at the time.

Remembering back, Judi half shouted and half barked at little Stella, "what you got in that box Moyssi?" That was the first time I ever heard Judy speak, nothing wrong with her. She was just plain ignorant and kept herself to herself, but obviously the situation of the prostrate Stella and the Matchbox proved too much for her to resist

It was right there and then the magic happened. It was then all ingredients were mixed together and continued forward producing a lifelong friendship between the misfits Judi, Lizzie and little Stella. To this day, I still wish we'd never forced Stella to open her little Matchbox only because of what she had inside the damn thing, The memory of it still fills me with utter revulsion, you see it was the remains of Stella's pet mouse Jerry, who was unfortunate enough to escape right into the paws and claws of the families pet cat Sylvester. I still remember the poor little thing lying there in its makeshift hospital bed, which unfortunately become its coffin all shaking and blooded.

I still blame Stella decades on for my lifelong phobia of dead things. However, from that day on the three of us became inseparable. There was also a firm pecking order, just like in all family dynamics. Judi was the father, I was the mother, and Stella became our child; meaning she did exactly what her makeshift parents told her to bloody do. Stella accepted it. Without question. Thinking back Jude was highly protective over the both of us. We had become her purpose in life, and low and behold her wrath if anyone got any idea in their heads to interfere or harm, her new found family. Judith Bromley aka (Judi-The-Jew) was fully prepared to protect us with her life, two and a half decades later she fulfilled that obligation, put it this way if she didn't, I wouldn't be here telling this story today, but as the old saying goes "that's another story". Completely.

Up until then, Judi only had one friend in the world, a massive angry looking dog called Sandy. Sandy gave her the freedom to roam the streets on her own in the middle of the night. No one in their right mind would approach that dog if they wanted to live. Granny Blanche was not at all happy with my new choice of friends. There wasn't a day that went by when I didn't arrive home bloodied or bleeding. I was often filthy dirty, with my beautiful expensive clothes ripped to shreds and covered in mud, after our adventures on the bombsites, a gift kindly left for Devonport's Boomer child by the German air forces nightly raids on its Devonport's famous dockyard.

My princess, lady like clothes were completely inappropriate for my new found escapades with my new gang. Can you imagine climbing a rock face, or exploring old tunnels in frilly petticoats? I used to dream of being free of those frills. All I wanted was to dress in jeans and T-shirt like Judi, who point blankly refused anything feminine at all. Poor little Stella, wore whatever she could get her hands on that day. If she was lucky, she got to wear the hand me downs that Judi provided, or what she could sneak out behind her mother's back, before wash day had arrived.

But I looked and felt like a right twat! It took in total about 12 of my legendary Billy Bunter tantrums to get my own way regarding my attire.

I found myself repeating word for word, the instructions from Judi that day, and that was to tell my Gran this. Graaaaaany, "I was playing handstands and climbing trees, and Stella noticed that a man, in a mac or rain coat? Was looking right up my skirt at my knickers!" Horrible lie, I know but it worked because my poor granny Blanche was mortified. In horror granny Blanche finally relented buying me my first pair of slacks, we'd called them leggings now. However, in those days, slacks had stirrups at the bottom to hook under the soles of your feet to prevent them from riding up the leg, Granny Blanche explained.

With just a few tiny harmless fibs I had got my way however she points blankly refused to remove the pink red and white ribbons from my frizzy hair, which were actually pointless because I had absolutely nothing to tie up? They were sort of just stuck to the side of my Afro. I suppose where she thought little girls ponytails should be poor gran did her best though.

The three of us explored everywhere. Me and Stella always obeying word for word the instructions from Judi. On this particular day Judi had decided in her wisdom, we were to leave our county on our own for the very first time. She planned and planned giving us a list of the essentials we would need to undertake and survive such a dangerous excursion. What I mean is gave me the list because poor Stella had very little resources to plunder from her humble home.

By my ample size it was evident my kitchen cupboards were overflowing with the good stuff. Obviously my job was to provide the food, understandable but not all that easy. Easy for kids now, however in the 60's there was no such thing as fast food, apart from fish and chips and then you still have to wait in line for it to be cooked!

I remember lying in my bed that night, racking my brains. Worrying myself sick that my friends were probably going to starve to death, because of my incompetence in not being able to provide transportable food. I remember having one shilling savings to my name, but I was going to need that for the ferry that connected Devon to the Mount Edgecombe estate in Cornwall. Stella's crossing was to be paid for by Judi, who informed us casually that she was just going to nick their ferry money from her mother's purse that night, after she came home after working in the pub and said that she had no chance of being caught because her mum Pat would be drunk. Ah the good old days when a barmaid could take her tip in drinks, lol.

However, Judi had given me absolutely no instructions on how I was to get the food? I had (up to that point) never stolen a single thing in my life, especially where food was concerned. Reason being, I had been practically force fed by my over protective grandmother, since the day I was born! Lots of Boomer children were.

By 11 o'clock that night I remember lying in my bed crying my eyes out worried sick that my best friends in the whole wide world were both going to starve to death and it was going to be my stupid fault! It was then in the blackness of that night I had my eureka moment. We're not just going to eat a snack the next day, our dinner was going to be soddin spectacular!

My morning started with the usual, "Goodbye Elizabeth" I'll see you later, from Gran as she departed for work. Like most of the children of the day, I was what you would call a latchkey kid. In other words, we took care of ourselves. Tradition of the time was to have the front door key suspended behind the letterbox on a piece of string, you pulled through the letterbox to lock the door on your way out and pushed back in through the letterbox. It made no sense then, and it makes no sense now, considering the fact a burglar would know exactly where your front door key was, if they wanted to rob you blind. We'd just as well left the door wide open. However, that's how things were done in them days.

There was not a chance in hell; I was going to have a wash that day. In fact to hurry the process along, the night before, I had decided to ditch my pyjamas and sleep in the clothes that would be needed for our excursion to Cornwall the next morning. Within a minute I was ready all that was needed was for me to collect our food and then wait for Judi to arrive, 9 o'clock she said she would call for me it was now 9:15! In all the years that I had known Judi she was never once on time and never early, unlike me who was never late.

The next task was to call for Stella, and that was a task in itself. It was actually was quite perilous, considering the fact that Stella's dad couldn't stand the sight of me or Judi. However, the sight of us both together could almost send him over the edge! In fact, Stella's dad hated everybody, me especially. I found out years later it wasn't exactly hatred because of my colour which we suspected at the time.

The real reason was the fact that every time he saw me, he lost a vast amount money on the races? In other words, I was a jinx. Funnily enough, he may have been the first person to think this, but he definitely wasn't the last person to say that about me! Granny Blanche used to say my Elizabeth could literally fall in shit and come up smelling of roses, but I don't hold out much hope for the poor sods with her. LOL.

Judy instructed me to call for Stella. I was always the one who had to do the calling, as Judi explained I had a bigger mouth than most and was the most likely to be heard. You see in Devonport calling for someone doesn't actually mean physically knocking on someone's front door, its literally calling by name the person you want up to or through a window of their house. "Calling for someone actually meant calling", Stella!

The day was doomed, and a disaster from the start. Not only was rain forecast, but Stella was wearing a flimsy little dress which was completely inappropriate for our day's vigorous excursion in the woods and forest of Mount Edgecombe Park. This led Judi to pontificate about the spare pair of shorts she brought with her claiming that they wouldn't keep Stella warm, but "least the poor little sod won't be showing her knickers." Knowing Stella's impoverished situation, it was always debatable whether she actually had any knickers on at all.

In my childhood days a water bottle was completely unheard of. In fact, the only time I ever saw a water bottle was in the old western movies only then it was called a canteen. Judi explained that we would need to find a toilet or a stream if we got thirsty and with that, we set off on our adventure leaving the safely and for me, especially the protection, of my beloved Devonport.

Taking the Cremyll Ferry was a short 15 minutes trip from Devon to Cornwall's Mount Edgcumbe Park all I could think of that day was, if my Gran could see me now she would absolutely kill me, but I couldn't care less. I was with my two best friends, wearing my new liberating slacks minus the 2 pink ribbons in my bloody hair! I was feeling as free as a bird that day, and remember the freedom like it was yesterday. Any consequences I was more than happy to suffer afterwards. Judi informed me and Stella that we will eat the dinner I was ordered to provide when we got there. Where there was, we had absolutely no idea. We just kept our mouths shut, and followed our leader blindly until we actually got to Judie's "there", of course.

I still remember the look of horror on Judy and Stella's face, the day we sat down for our well-earned lunch. You see my plan the day before; to sneak in to Granny Blanches kitchen, and make a pile of cheese and pickle sandwiches, to grab a few biscuits out of Grandmas favourite biscuit tin, then create a perfect lunchtime snack for the three of us.

Id managed sneak into the kitchen successfully however to my horror when I opened the fridge there was no cheese. Then I opened the bread bin, there was absolutely no bread to be seen! You wouldn't have even got a teaspoon out of the pickle jar in all honesty I was horrified at the fact we had no food in the house, meaning that Granny Blanche was probably dead, or had been kidnapped, because there was always food? But also, the fact my two friends were going to go hungry on our special day out all because of Lizzie the jinx's incompetence!

I remember sitting in our kitchen that morning forcing myself to come up with ideas on how I could feed Judi, Stella and myself on our excursion. When I noticed a brown paper bag sitting at the very bottom of the fridge. On investigation, I found three of the most perfect lamb chops I had ever seen, not giving a thought in hell on how I was going to be able to cook three lamb chops, plus the three large raw potatoes I decided to add to our meal? I remember thinking cabbage and carrots a bit too much for a camp meal so decided to leave them out.

But I was looking at the world and the debacle of my situation through a child's eyes. However not just any child, I was looking through Lizzies eyes, which as you may have guessed by now could prove to be a disaster. Well, they were not pleased. In fact, they were not pleased at all. Judy flu into a blind rage and little Stella started crying, when they saw my effort of a packed lunch. With that, the discussion was over, and our adventure of a lifetime was over, way before it had started. I couldn't argue it was entirely my fault, but how the hell was I to know when Granny Blanche did the grocery shopping!

I didn't say a word to my companions all the way home from Cornwall to Plymouth, However, on the ferry crossing back over The Tamar River I had one of my all too common, but disastrous lightbulb moments. Unfortunately, yes it was the same sort of lightbulb moment that carried on way into my adult hood. However, at the time it was just another one of my many so called good ideas, I remember trying to redeem myself by telling my friends my new plan.

On the Plymouth side of the Cremyll Ferry there was a small corner shop. It was there I purchased my first box of matches explaining my plan to my comrades and was delighted when Judi said it might work, and little Stella's mood seemed to pick up immediately. My plan was to cook Granny Blanche's prime lamb chops in the public toilet. Reason being there was going to be lots and lots of paper to start the fire needed for a barbecue I explained, we had the chops, check! We had the matches, check! A few sticks we had gathered off the side of the hedge row, check! With that amount of planning and preparation what could possibly go wrong?

Unfortunately, this was one of my brain storming moments that almost got us killed; the good news was the toilet paper and sticks made an excellent fire. Unfortunately, the bad news was I set the wooden toilet stall on fire as well. Filling the toilet and our young lungs with thick black smoke! If you've ever experienced smoke inhalation, it's not a very pleasant experience at all. In fact, it's a bloody terrifying and painful experience for anybody unfortunately caught in the path of a fire.

I remember Granny Blanche crying once again

"Elizabeth this time you have gone too bloody far ", to tell the truth I was so traumatised Grans ranting speech was going in one ear and out the other. However, I do remember her sobbing words like they are going to end up "putting her away in a minute" and you're grounded, and that feeling of being kicked in the teeth on hearing the words   I'm confiscated your transistor radio! Blah blah blah blah blah! In other words, I was up shit creek without a paddle. The worst bit was I had absolutely no excuse this time; I just had to suck up the punishment and take the medicine!

At this point I was in the biggest shit I've ever been in my life. In the end my only pathetic defence was" it's not like anybody died did they!" That was mine and my two best childhood friends many adventures, especially over Mount Edgecombe Park. After disobeying Granny Blanche orders, hundreds of times I took that little Ferry boat to freedom.

My childhood years passed, and my dressing downs, punishments and penalties grew in intensity. Apparently, the apple never falls far from the tree; yes, I had turned into my mother, the delinquent, Shirley Rose. With my grandmother often proclaiming, she should have "knocked seven bells of shit out of me!" when I was younger, an old Navy saying. She carried on with her normal drunken character assassinations of me, accusing me of making her old before her time, and turning her hair bloody white with anguish. The best one, wait for it, I was turning her to drink? That was a good one Lol.

I was slowly, but surely getting the blame for every single one of my Grans downfalls. I remember her once falling to her knees with her hands open wide, drunkenly pleading to her God why can't she, meaning me, be like the perfect Jilly Cusack? I remember getting another proverbial clip around the ear after claiming loudly that her request was impossible for even God to grant considering the fact that Jill was probably only so perfectly normal because she had a decent normal family bringing. Unlike me!

Gran was absolutely outraged! Bless her. However, I think I may have hit a raw nerve and often wonder what a behavioural psychologist would have to say on the matter. Considering the fact this socially inept, tiny illiterate woman who wouldn't even say boo to a goose, seemed to have produced not one but two totally extroverted rebellious out of control daughters? Who technically, in all honesty, absolutely didn't appear to give a shit what other people thought of their bad, outlandish behaviour. Could it be genetic? Probably?

Apparently, if you want a conflict free life, you leave religion and politics out of the equation. At the grand old age of 11, I found out that my perfect little gang of three looked very likely to be ripped apart. Due to the fact that our poor little Stella was a Catholic. You see Judi and I were brought up as Protestants in the Faith of the Church of England, meaning by the age of eleven, I had to go to a separate school from our Stella.

Me and Judi were enrolled at Devonport Secondary Modern, after failing the Eleven plus Exam, me miserably! In other words, to be educated in the factory fodder educational system of Devonport Secondary Modern School. It was located on the outskirts of the very beautiful Victorian

Devonport Park. Stella was enrolled into Saint Peters Catholic School located off the Octagon, an area not far from Plymouths notorious red light district and home to the hundreds of rowdy drinking dens of Union Street.

Our poor little Stella was on her own. We were worried sick, but there was nothing we could do to protect her. We hated her dad even more than we did before. To made matters worse, Judi said that he had probably done it on purpose in order to break us up! In all fairness to Mr Moisey, I've never met a Protestant Greek Cypriot family there are probably lots but I've never met one in my lifetime. With that, we resigned ourselves to the fact that we were going to have to spend the next five "school years" apart like it or lump it. That's exactly what was going to happen.

"This is the first time in my forty seven years of teaching have I ever had to authorise six of the best, (caning) to a female pupil. "Yep, you guessed it didn't take long for me to go down in somebody's history! I remember that day vividly mainly because my wet sop of a headmaster was leaning on the other side of his desk, dressed in his full educational black gowns and mortarboard, he was crying like a big baby. I remember thinking Gods, truth man why the hell are you crying it's me who's not going to be able to sit down for a bloody week! However, I was a bit taken back when he said on the "left hand please headmistress" knowing the boys got the stick on the ass.

The old bitter spinster was brought down especially to administer a "female to female" corporal punishment, I remember thinking the old twat didn't even have the guts to do it himself! And what was my heinous crime? You're going to love this one lol.

My favourite part of the day was to escape into the open space of the beautiful Victorian gardens of Devonport Park. Even though we had been warned not to wonder there alone especially at night, mainly because of the hundreds of graphic stories of the dirty old men hiding behind the many trees and bushes throughout the park. We were told horror stories or perverts traveling far and wide in order to attack unsuspecting females of Devonport However, we the fresh faced recruits upon arrival at Devonport Sec received an extra warning not only concerning the hordes of dirty old men ready to pounce and rob us of our virginity, but also the perils of mixing with the pupils of the all-boys school (Devonport high school for boys).

The school was the cooking pot of the young upper/middle-class privileged lads who had all been schooled often privately, to a high academic level, enough to pass their 11+ exam. These privileged few, were destined to become the doctors, pilots and engineers of the future. The one thing I have learned throughout my long and colourful life is those Grans old wives saying that "opposites' attract", to be absolutely spot on!   Especially where complete opposites are concerned.

You see the posh boys from the very old and distinguished Devonport high School for boys, and the far from posh council estate girls from the factory fodder Devonport secondary modern got on like a house on fire! You could almost feel the juvenile sexual tension when the two groups met, normally around the tennis courts, having absolutely nothing in common apart from the fact that good looking boys and very hot the teenage girls were meeting up. Nothing in common my back side lol.

The boys of our mixed school normally stayed well away, preferring football to the posh boy's rugby. You see, the boys of my school were well used to us females, preferring to spend their dinnertime break without our interference. Many were glad to be rid of us, joking loudly that they were glad to be bloody rid of us interfering loud and moody girls. Quite unlike the posh boys from the single sex Devonport high who technically couldn't get enough of us. In fact, to put it plainly, they were absolutely gagging for it!

Unlike the boys from my school these guys didn't mind, nor should I say didn't feel embarrassed about showing a high level of sexual interest either. I for one enjoyed the unselfconscious and relaxed attitude of these upper-class posh boys. Even at that early age, I had the don't-beat-about no nonsense let's get on with it attitude, as I've said previously I'm black or white, or hot or cold, and can't stand pissing about in the middle.

However, there were a few who I found to be damn right arrogant in their attitude towards us lower class, working-class girls. The girls from my school were far from stupid, leaving these stuck up snobs out of any fraternisation. No kiss, no cuddle, and defiantly no how's-your–father in the many secluded parts of Devonport Park. I'm still friends with a few of the good ones now.

I remember the day vividly. I also remember being extremely annoyed at Judi for receiving yet another half an hour midday detention for some misdemeanour I forget. I remember my walk up the leafy sunlit tunnel of overhanging trees on the short journey to my favourite park bench, and I also remember him the arrogant little sod! At the time I was desperately stuffing my face with my favourite chocolate bar. It was literally on that turning point of turning to mush, I don't know about you but I've always preferred my chocolate, cold and crispy not soft and runny.

I unfortunately the day was hot, and I'd pushed my luck waiting for Judi, knowing she would soon follow. So, when I heard "hey big jugs wanna see my balls" it knocked me completely off my flow causing me to drop a lump of almost liquid chocolate on my pristine white cotton blouse! Regarding the chocolate situation any normal nice girl would have probably said, oh dear me, what have I done? But I was not a normal nice girl, was I? I was livid and literally exploded into profanities, I was absolutely literally spitting mad, especially when I saw my would-be assailant.

I can see him now with a face I can only describe as a flat dinner plate! He was probably one of the ugliest boys I'd ever seen in my life, who had obviously heard the tantalising and exaggerated stories of the promiscuous, easy going council estate girls. I can imagine hiding around the corner listening to the sexual antics of the more popular boys from his school, and decided to have a go and try his luck. Unfortunately for him, he'd just picked on the wrong person to be his victim, me! Black Lizzie who had a temper like a Torpoint chicken, in other words I was bat-shit-crazy to say the least.

I was almost 15 by now and well used to warding off unwelcome attention from not only school boys, but also real grown up men. In other words, perverts, who prey on young girls. So, a chubby faced rampant adolescent, who had obviously no one to ramp on, was about to be swatted like the proverbial fly! I was just about to abandon my chocolate bar for good and beat the living daylights out of him when Judi emerged like a cat from the undergrowth behind him.

It reminded me of one of those wild life programs, when the predator hides in plain sight, Judi was quietly closing in when she got to about 10 feet behind him, I remembered thinking, oh shit, this is not going to end well for you now Laddie! What happened next? I can only describe as a titanic tug of war between Judi and my uncouth Romeo. From what I could make out to be a pair of boys school trousers, after darting out of the bushes she had snatched his school pants at lightning speed out of the top of his PE/sports bag.

I honestly couldn't stop laughing, especially when Judi started to be dragged at least 10 feet along the gravel path. She would not let go, not on your Nelly. She may have been skinny, but when that girl got a grip on something she didn't easily let go. However, the path was made of gravel and small stones I knew that if she didn't let go, there was a possibility her legs would be ripped to pieces. I remember thinking, over my dead body was I going to let anyone especially the likes of him hurt her, after all she was my best friend in the whole wide world, I had no option but to storm in.

Between the two of us, and a lot tugging and pulling, we managed to rip the trousers literally in half! The battle with my flat faced ugly opponent, who was by now screaming like boy who had never even possessed a pair of balls, was almost over! His flat face had turned bright pink and was now crying like the big fat baby he obviously was inside. Yelling at the top of his voice, "you're going to rip my new trousers you effin bitch!" With that Judi screaming back well "soddin let go you fat twat!" Oh my God what a kerfuffle lol. However, with me joining the medley, it didn't take long to rip the trousers off him. With that we ran off triumphantly.

Judi prided herself on being cool, and never showing too much emotion especially in conflict. But oh no, not that day. I remember her running off, waving his trousers in the air, leaving the once randy, now thoroughly humiliated schoolboy, sobbing on his backside. As an act of compassion, plus the fact his school pant were of absolutely of no use to us, we tied his trousers to the top of the children's climbing frame, and with that we made our way back to school.

Well, that was our side of the story, however, however the randy dirty little sod of a school boy's story was completely different, of courses! When he arrived back at school minus his trousers and now replaced with nothing more than a pair of flimsy football shorts, which was a serious misdemeanour in those days, may I add? He had obviously decided the only way to save himself the embarrassment of the true events of the day, creating the most traumatic and dramatic excuse he could.

His side of the story was a large black girl, and her skinny white mate were so overtaken with desire at the sight of him, sitting quietly doing his homework under a tree, like lightning we had pounded out of nowhere. We ripped off his trousers, such was the level of our desire, and it was only by a stroke of luck, and by the skin of his teeth, he had managed to escape our rampant advances, I couldn't believe my ears when I found myself standing in front of my headmaster, being accused of sexual assault.

I must have ranted and raged for about an hour in my defence. You'll never guess why they actually believed him. He was the son of a local doctor, and I was from a poor council estate of course. Remember for centuries the rich have been regarded as good, and the poor bad, and are untrustworthy right? Resulting in me, becoming the first girl in the school's history, plus ruining my headmaster's long career, of never having to order a female to receive six of the best! Judi being one of the hundreds of white girls who frequented the park was hard to identify.

It was 1975. The war in Vietnam had just ended. It was finally over for the millions affected by it. In my opinion, the only good thing to come out of that war was the music of the time. It inspired in some to produce music and lyrics, bordering on genius! Us, the Boomer kids, we were on the receiving end of something that was truly magical. Then followed by the disco Revolution and music produced in America's Detroit Motor-city along with the Philadelphia rhythms, all produced without a synthesiser insight. I truly believe that Boomer child was part of something that will never be repeated artistically.

As thick as two short planks, was my only description for Judi, who obviously could not stand the thought of me, single-handedly, taking the blame for her actions that day. The fool only rocked up to the receptionist office, and confessed to being my accomplice in the vicious sexual assault on the most undesirable twat on the planet becoming the second girl in our Head Masters long history of teaching to receive a six of the best. The beating also administered by his female henchman.

That was the day I confirmed to myself that no teacher was ever going to be allowed to lay one finger on me again, or any children, if I ever was to have any? Reason being 1, because it bloody hurt for a start! 2, I suspected they both may have had perverted intentions! Even at my young age I believed then and still do that there was a certain level of deviancy needed to administer such a punishment on a child.

Traditionally, boys were caned on the trouser backside. Us girls on the palms of our hands. Normally punishment always performed in front of a witness. Normally in front of the whole class, as an added deterrent for bad behaviour adding to your humiliation. However, these practices were only guidelines. Guidelines to be interpreted, or in many cases abused by the educator, the people who had power over these young minds and bodies at the time.

I believe it was three separate incidents that took place within less than a week. That put-pay to the disgraceful and humiliating practice of corporal punishment in my school. I'm going to be clinical here in my descriptions as I have a tendency to become emotional and angry when thinking about those so called teachers, many I believe to be sadists hiding in plain sight! Here's my reason why guys.

Less than a week after our so-called rampant sexual encounter in the park, a boy named William was caned (on the hand) by an enthusiastic teacher Who apparently got so carried away with excitement, missed his target bringing the bamboo cane down upon poor Billy's tender wrist with such force it snapped, crushed or bruised the artery causing poor Billy's arm to swell up to almost the size of an elephants foot, so I was told by an excited witness.

It's been described to me that Poor Billy was stretchered off the hospital, screaming his head off being followed by a very guilty and frightened looking teacher. Leaving Williams parents no option but to phone the police because there was absolutely no chance they would get any kind of justice from the educational authority that approved such punishments, Leading The so-called teacher to be formally interviewed by the Devon and Cornwall police department.

The second incident was less painful but for more sinister, this time concerning a girl, I'm going to call her Susan to protect her identity. She was also caned. However, highly unusually in private by a male teacher. Not on the hand no, but on back side! It gets worse, not on a clothed backside like the boys, but unbelievably on her bare backside. God forbid. Susan's parents understandably phoned the police, and this teacher was arrested and formally charged.

Finally, the third incident that week this time of a boy named Colin. This resulted in a teacher being attacked in the car park by Colin's father who broke his jaw permanently also removing three of the teachers teeth. Once again, the police were called, this time not for the teacher. However, the parent was left off with a warning, after the full story of why he was driven to such an act of violence was revealed.

And that was the three strike rule. This was a cruel game. Some of the teachers liked to play on us.

This form of Corporal punishment did not involve the traditional bamboo cane; it involved one of the heavy wooden rulers every teacher possessed. In those days, a cruel game involving a teacher bringing the sharp edge of the ruler down on the tips of your fingers. Trust me; this punishment really did bloody hurt if you were unlucky enough to be on the receiving end of this torture.

The game was played once you placed your flat hand palm down on the desk. The teacher would then strike down at full force. Now if you were fast or lucky enough to remove your hands out of its path three times your punishment would be cancelled. How bloody horrific was that? I witnessed children with their nails missing and finger tips left black and blue by those bloody perverted sadists.

We spent our days running the daily gauntlet of the proverbial clip around the ear, which basically involved being slapped at fall force on the side of the head with the flat of a teacher's hand. Or finding yourself being dragged by ear just because your teacher was in a bad mood that day! Finally, their favourite which also involves the use of a lump of wood. The throwing of the black board rubber!

This required the teacher to take aim at his desired target and throw a lump of hardwood approximately 4 inches long covered in felt at the head of his desired victim! It was like an Olympic sport to these bloody psychos, not only did it hurt a lot; it very often left bruising on the unlucky child's head or body. I remember it exploding in a massive cloud of white chalk when it found its target covering the poor kid from head to toe in white powder.

From what I remember of my school days very few teachers were kind and non-violent. This sort of behaviour had been a traditional practice in the UK for decades with educators holding extreme power over our young bodies and minds. However Very few children complained to their parents, knowing they would probably receive a similar punishment for being naughty in school, because teachers don't lie, do they? In my memory they lied and did far worse.

Do you remember when I talked about my experiences, of me returning back to Learning and my difficulty understanding, certain terminology and concepts concerning political history, and how a lecturer made the concept of "A revolution" easily understandable for me and that was to think of a revolution as change or changing and that I remembered someone writing that it only needed one act of defiance to start that revolution. Well, I witnessed that act of defiance from an unassuming young boy, who, by saying the word no ended the barbaric practices of Corporal punishment in my school for good and his name was

Edwin (Charlie) Pearce.

Unbeknown to young Edwin, at the time his one act of defiance started a trend among the children of my school, the term that no means no., No you are not going to hit me! No, I do not want to be touched by you in any shape or form. No, I will not comply with your orders in public, or private. Finally, I do not agree, and will not submit to your punishments! In other words, "piss off teacher".

Many children said these words, or words to that effect, without, temper or tantrum. To be perfectly honest, the teachers did not know what to do. Their reign of terror was over. Their power was diminishing with every act of passive defiance, However, it was replaced by brutal after school detentions I remember twenty minutes into an hour long detention being exhausted, after writing line after line "I-AM-STUPID" for of my misdemeanours and in absolute torture, thinking I would rather take the six of the best on the bare ass, even though it hurt like bloody hell.

I only ever remember two other girls who were caned at Devonport secondary Modern named Diane Friend and Denise Kingcombe.

Both, may I add, were sometimes extremely naughty. Put it this way, they had to be if they wanted to be friends of mine! They were also both Devonport Maids. However, from a completely different area of Devonport from mine and Judi's, which was Mount wise. Their area was the pottery key area of Devonport.

It was equally deprived.

However, their traditions and tribalism match mine and Judi's upbringing. The area is also deeply embedded in Plymouths Naval history. Once again, the areas existence revolved around the Tamar River, and claimed ownership of a couple of century old ferries, which carried goods and vehicles back and forth over the Plymouth to Cornwall border and vice versa.

The Torpoint ferry was a much larger operation, compared to our tiny passenger only ferry, which only carried foot passengers only to the Majestic, Mount Edgecombe estate in Cornwall.

Diane and Denise were also a double act. Where Diane went Denise Would not to be far behind. Apart from location and the fact they were a double act like us, and we all went to the same school, these were the only similarities these Pottery Key girls had to me, black Lizzie and Judi the Jew.

That was evident by the lack of nastiness they had. In fact, looking back over the years, these two girls didn't seem to have a bad bone in their body. Put it this way, they didn't have a hidden dark side like the crafty and sometimes dark Lizzie and Judi.

It was only last week I got a fit in my head (spontaneous idea) in Devonport language, deciding to visit Diane in the little café, she runs in the Marlborough Street area of Devonport called simply, Rosie Leighs café (PL1 4AH). After all these years I expected, but was still delighted, when her eyes lit up, recognising me instantly when I walked in. Keeping in the tradition of all Devonport homecomings. But what took me completely by surprise was the appearance of Denise! but I shouldn't have been surprised that her old mate and partner in crime wasn't far behind even after all these years, however, I shouldn't have been surprised because it's just the Devonport Way, owing to the fact, when Devonport people make friends they become sort of a family it's a lifelong commitment. They of course were a lot older however the banter and connection between them and me was exactly how I remember, the only thing missing was Judi who had sadly passed of the Cancer a few years ago, I could feel her close to us though.

Years later, when I had my own children, I remembered all this. Deciding rather than forcing my children to eat their greens, I gave them the simple choice of basically to eat, or don't eat. Letting them decide their own actions, as hot headed as I was, I despised the idea of parental smacking. Put it this way, it never worked for me, apart from making me even more obstinate and hard to control that is. Out of my five children, two have never been smacked by me ever; both are well balanced funny and extremely kind individuals.

Two of their siblings received only ever one light tap on the back of their legs for the crime of disappearing into Plymouth city centre for five, of the worst hours of my entire life. With the stress, almost putting me in hospital. However, two taps was all I could manage. I only administered the taps because Granny Blanche had insisted on some kind of a punishment, warning that if I didn't, they're wandering would not stop, and I could possibly end up losing them forever.

The final child received two smacks at different intervals for stealing sweet money, when he was old enough to know better. However, his criminal career started way before when this tiny terror was just 5 months old. I was shopping in Woolworths, and took my eyes off him for a second that was all that was needed for him to snatch a massive bar of

Cadburys chocolate that was conveniently stacked on a low level shelf, perfect grabbing distance for a baby!

By the time Granny Blanche had noticed, he had already consumed practically half the chocolate bar, silver paper and all, he was absolutely covered in the brown sticky goo from head to toe I almost burst out laughing when I saw. It had matted his hair. It was in his eyes, his ears, all over his pram and cot blankets. Granny Blanche was livid, her description of the scene was, "he's absolutely blinking plastered in it! " Granny was so furious she point blankly refused to push his pram, stating that we "looked like we were off a soddin council estate!

Reflections

By now it must be evident that my grandmother Blanche constructed a massive part of my life. Reading back over my story, it is pretty obvious I was destined to follow my own stubborn path not anybody else's. Like every Journey we undertake, I found myself traversing the easy ground, hills and potholes, However, as I travelled forward from point A to B, I found that my journey was often broken into unrelated, interconnecting connecting segments, of life bubbles.

Presenting those bubbles like a new jigsaw puzzle, broken segments that fit together perfectly to make the whole picture, sometimes after I'd done the work, sometimes by doing nothing at all. The making of me in other words. It's showed me where I'd rested, scanning the clear horizon for the good times ahead, more than often leaving me shaking my head over the times I had wasted by just ploughing on aimlessly. One of the greatest lessons I learned by reflecting, is that it was impossible to force life, it showed me that the only thing me or any of us can do for that matter is to just sit back, be patient. In other words, wait.

The best part was, finding myself lucky enough and in exactly the right position where the sun shone on me for no reason at all letting fate do its job. Then finding myself rolling in happiness, just like the night I met the Welshman. Who would have thought that such happiness could be brought about by a series of stupid mistakes that had happened that night? I shudder to think if I had refused Roxanne's demands to go out on the town that night, I could have denied myself a lifetime of happiness.

Hopefully by now, my personality has been fully revealed. Revealing at heart I am a playful spirit, coming over to the world as a bit of a joker. A person who doesn't like to take life too seriously. However, some of the people who know me well have described this part of my character as flawed, a bravado put in place when I'm-not wanting, or not ready to face up to the truth. They are probably right because more than once, I have found myself so battered down by life storms that were so powerful, so destructive in temperament they almost broke in to me in two. On more than one occasion those storms descended on me so bloody hard, bashing me left right and centre. But would I show my frailties to the world outside would I hell!

My Gran used to warn people to be careful, and to never underestimate my playful good nature, saying that I "was very deep". She said that while everyone was laughing and joking at my antics, I would be casually but expertly extracting every single bit of information about their lives, and would use it against them if I was ever crossed. I think the old bat was wrong about that, because I've always just

Seen myself as a good listener, a woman who enjoyed putting people at ease with my light hearted banter. However, I'm the classic elephant in the room who never forgets.

The writing down of my story has enlightened me to the fact, no matter how bad things got, or how bad I was feeling, the one thing I did without fail was carry on moving forward. As far as I'm concerned, the past is in the past so leave it there. When times did get hard, I always found myself "pulling my socks up" just cracking on in life.

But I don't see myself as unique, and definitely not special. I'm just like you and the rest of the world, I did what I've have to do to survive the difficult, sometimes painful situations life lobs at us from time to time. I could ramble over and over into a self-gratifying chest thumping speech on the tactics I used, and how I grew strong when facing my demons. However, in truth, I realise I've faced nothing unique enough to class myself, as poor little abandoned Lizzie, and I certainly wasn't brave or courageous, on many occasions I've ran like the wind in order to hide from the world and balled my eyes out more times than I've had hot dinners!

In my stubbornness, selfishness or just plain stupidity I just cracked on putting one size 7 boot foot, in front of the other, day-in day-out exactly like billions of human beings who live on this planet have had to do, just doing my very best in order to survive and hopefully thrive. Granny Blanche used to say, "I would rather have a thief than a liar" When questioned why? She said you can always catch and redeem a thief, but a liar is always a liar!

She said a thief is a thief out of necessity whether it's out of hardship or greed. However, a liar is a deceiver that could rob another person of their self-worth describing them as the lowest of the low! That's Granny Blanches firm opinion, and for once I fully agree with her because I hate bloody liars with every bone in my body!

The irony is by telling the truth like I do, can often get you singled out as one of the bad guys and this has proved a real pain in the arse and one of my biggest downfalls in life, when opening my big mouth in defence of the truth, and also responsible for getting me into serious trouble more times than I've had hot dinners. In the past, it's seen me cast out, ostracised or worse on many occasions. Here's a good old fashion life hack if you really truly want to hurt someone.

The solution is as easy as taking candy from the proverbial baby don't mess about

Just-tell-em-the-bloody-truth, then stand back take cover because all bloody hell is about to break lose! The truth can be the most destructive weapon in your arsenal, but be warned as the old saying goes some people can't handle the truth.

However, at times, I can be an expert liar. I hold my hands up, because I am guilty of telling what I call the "kind lies" or what Granny Blanche called, the little white lies. These lies are sometimes necessary, when the act of telling the real truth could hurt an innocent or flatten someone's confidence, in Devonport we would say "why burst their bubble". There's no need for it.

Situations like when your best friend has an arse so fat even Nelly the elephant would look slim in comparison, why would you feel the need to ruin their day? Think what could I possible gain from it. If asked, "Does my bum look big in this?" I do what every good husband in the western world would do, and just lie. On many occasions, I've had to cross my fingers behind my back and said words to the effect; no you look great babe, all the time being very tempted to say are you kidding me? Your gigantic solar eclipsing, equator measuring fat arse is absolutely enormous!

But that would be cruel; it would be spiteful and ruin their day. Especially right after they'd spent probably the most painful hour of their life squeezing into their skin tight leather look leggings. No, I just couldn't do it, I can be bad but not that bad. However, I can't guarantee I would be able to keep my mouth shut over the apparition of a massive camel toe! The worst wardrobe failure in the entire world, even I have to draw the line at that unforgivable crime. May I add a crime I can safely say I've never been guilty of in any shape or form! Granny Blanche would say sometimes, "You have to be cruel to be kind" in this case be very cruel, take pictures if you have to, but stop them!

Granny Blanche with her many fables and old wives tales have left me completely and utterly baffled at times, especially as a child. However, as an adult, I've re-evaluated many of them such as the comparison between the thief and the liar?

I've come to the conclusion what she meant to say is, people can change after a bad act.

Like the case of me being born of mix race, with some older members of my family who would, by today's standards of political correctness, be classed as a racist or bigots.

However, time has shown their attitude wasn't down to the fact they disliked black people and people from different culture or races, it was down to one simple fact they just didn't know any people from different races from themselves which is a completely different kettle of fish.

The love and attention I received after my arrival is proof and testament that every single one of them changed their opinion on race regarding me being taken into the fold, and protection of this very loving but very white family is one of the reasons I thrived. Because I was "different, they became overprotective. Constantly on the lookout to make sure I wasn't bullied or left out because of my colour. It was their love and support that gave me bucket loads of confidence, probably too much on many occasions.

I've often been classed of being "too big for my boots", in other words, arrogant.

The great matriarch's of the family, Granny Hill, Granny Blanche's mother and my great grandmother, direct descendants of the distinguished Tremaine family, who owned the lost Gardens of Heligan estate. May I add a woman not to be tangled with; it was she who ordered the entire family to "never take their eyes off me for a second". Saying words to the effect, she (me) didn't ask to be born, and it's not my fault I was black! Seeing my mixed race as some kind of a handicap.

This resulted in the entire family entertaining and granting my every whim, basically what Lizzie wanted Lizzie got, like Blanche, she worshipped the ground I walked on, I was spoiled rotten and acted accordingly. Yes, I was a monster.

That's my blood family (they did their best) however I'd been lucky enough to hit the jackpot in life not once but twice simply by being born in Devonport and also becoming a true Devonport maid. The people of Devonport could be rightly described as more of a clan or tribe rather than just the inhabitancy of an inner city council estate, similar in a way to the members of the Amish Community, if one person needed a barn erected the whole community were prepared to roll up their sleeves get their hands blooded and dirty to help build it. In other words, you are never on your own in a community like Devonport, you are truly blessed to be born in an environment where no one would ever be allowed to go cold or hungry, God forbid if anyone from the "out-side", dared to harm a hair on your head.

I was smack bang, due to my "racial disability" I was right in the middle of their attention as well! Now that's living, that's thriving not just surviving looked over by every single member of my community, nothing like most of the more well-off members of the western world, who keep to themselves but fingering your bank statement once a month can be a lonely life.

Gran used to say "you can't eat money", I still have absolutely no idea what she meant by that particular fable but I'd have a bloody good try…

I'm still in contact with practically all my old school friends. How many people can say that in this day and age? Today it's just a short car journey from my home in Cornwall back to Devonport, and example is, it had been years since I saw my old friend Gina Bromley, Judies older sister. If my memory serves me right about five years, I think. When I popped my head through her open window and called "All-right Gene", remember that I said Devonport people don't ever knock on doors they just call, no fanfare, no explanation. However, I was greeted with an "alright Liz I'll put the kettle on" and that was it, that's how we are, and that's what Devonport's people have always been like. They don't care what colour you are, where you've been, or how much money you have in the bank. They would say, you can stick all that up your ass you're either Devonport or you're not.

I've talked about my experiences of returning back into learning and my difficulty understanding certain terminology and concepts because of my lack of formal education. At first I had big problems understanding lots of things, especially political history. Very often I knew the answer but I just couldn't get it out in a way that anyone could understand. I was just about to give up and jack it all in when I was asked to explain the concept of "a revolution", all I could think of was the ordinary people get so pissed off they have a riot burn everything kill all the rich people and then live happily ever after, wrong!

Now try to think of a revolution as change or a change brought on by an action of the people or a person. I remembered something by Gandhi writing that it only needed one act of defiance to start that revolution. In other words, something to stop these violent teachers from inflicting harm on children, without the need of the kids parents knocking their teeth out in the school car park. It was obvious something had to be done, plus all that crap sayings like "it didn't do me any harm" because it did to many not just a few.

After all the complaining and phone calls to the police,

By saying that simple word (NO) he ended the barbaric practices of Corporal punishment in my school, all because of Edwin "Charlie" Pearce.

Who became my lifelong friend, (the boy who said no) who set a trend, because after him we all said that simple word no!

Taking away the teachers power over our young bodies.

I've been rabbiting on for so long I've even started to piss myself off with my ramblings, meaning I'm going to wrap this story up for now. On my book cover, I wrote about me being racially bullied and abused, the horrible truth is I really was, with no exaggeration, horribly and violently on many occasions.

However, this happened only when I wandered, and left the protection of my family and the Devonport clan, who to this day still love and over protect me. I actually blame them for encouraging my outrageous behaviour!

The reason I wrote this book was the last but not least one of my Granny Blanches favourite sayings. "You're only dead as long as you're forgotten".

The reality is an old and wise one, we all need to live and love now because in a hundred years' time, nobody's going to give a crap..

For my Gran!

Blanche Victory Peace Hill, 1919

AKA Granny Blanche, a fisherman's daughter.

DEVONPORT MAID
BY
LIZZIE KHALIL

Freya Beavis ©

Printed in Dunstable, United Kingdom

64558768R00147